MOTHER's MESSAGE IN A BOTTLE

Loving Letters for Life

edited by
Tyler Hayden

NIMBUS PUBLISHING

PUBLISHING

NIMBUS.CA

Nimbus Publishing Limited
3731 Mackintosh St, Halifax, NS B3K 5A5
(902) 455-4286 nimbus.ca

Printed and bound in Canada

NB1142

Design: Peggy Issenman, Peggy & Co. Design

Library and Archives Canada Cataloguing in Publication

Mother's message in a bottle : loving letters for life / edited by Tyler Hayden.
Issued in print and electronic formats.
  ISBN 978-1-77108-192-4 (pbk.).—ISBN 978-1-77108-193-1 (pdf).—
  ISBN 978-1-77108-194-8 (mobi).—ISBN 978-1-77108-195-5 (html)
1. Mother and child. 2. Mothers—Correspondence.
I. Hayden, Tyler, 1974-, editor of compilation

HQ759.M887 2014   306.874'3   C2013-908112-7
                                            C2013-908113-5

 Canada Council   Conseil des arts
for the Arts   du Canada

Nimbus Publishing acknowledges the financial support for its publishing activities from the Government of Canada through the Canada Book Fund (CBF) and the Canada Council for the Arts, and from the Province of Nova Scotia through Film & Creative Industries Nova Scotia. We are pleased to work in partnership with Film & Creative Industries Nova Scotia to develop and promote our creative industries for the benefit of all Nova Scotians.

For my wife, Laurie.

Laurie, you are such an amazing person. I can't believe my good fortune to have found you. I searched from coast to coast to find my soulmate, only to donate some time and energy to Lunenburg High and have the most wonderful woman walk into my life and live just down the road. You and I have taken so many adventures—some adrenaline filled and spontaneous, others planned and relaxing. But there has never been a journey more beautiful and meaningful than that of you ushering our daughters into this world.

Laurie, you are such an amazing mom. The way you love, the sacrifices you have made, and wisdom you share—I am in awe of you. It brings peace and strength to my heart helping you care for and love our children, and the countless others you reach out to through your work and community involvement.

This world is a better place because of you. Thank you for letting me join you on your magnificent journey. I love you.

I've got a good mother,
and her voice is what keeps me here.
Feet on ground,
Heart in hand,
Facing forward,

— "Good Mother," Jann Arden and Robert Foster, 1994

Contents

Preface

I remember the moment I learned what it means to be a great mother. It was a couple of weeks into being a new parent, when my wife and I had a visit from the public health nurse …

Here is a bit of the back story.

In Nova Scotia you are invited to "parent school" to learn to be a good parent. We watched videos, had discussions, and had burning questions answered. Our teacher was a public health nurse named Sue, and she was a pretty amazing person. Part of the class involved her coming to our home to "check in" (or up) on us a few weeks after our baby came home.

Here's where the story gets a bit sordid.

My wife and I decided in her eighth month of pregnancy to buy a "new" home. Actually, it was a dilapidated 250-year-old Cape Cod with rotten sills, broken windows, and one nasty bathroom. It was perfect, or so we thought. Except for that winter day I had to shovel the snowdrift out of our kitchen because the door didn't close properly—but that's another story.

Our house wasn't exactly…how do you say…like the pictures we saw in parenting class of babies at their homes. Needless to say, we loved our house, and my wife had done a great job of making it perfect for our baby.

Then the stress started.

We knew that Sue was coming. Reality hit and Laurie and I started to stress about the house and what the nurse would think. *That* sleepless night was caused by the stress rather than the new baby. Questions reeled in our heads: "Will Sue take our baby because of our unfit house? Will she tell us we have to move out because this place appears unfit for a baby?" And so much more 4:00 A.M. self talk.

Just before the nurse walked in, we did a final check of the house for proper installation of baby gates, safety plugs in sockets, and fresh batteries in the baby monitor. We felt it was as good as it would get.

Then the nurse walked in with a scale, binders, and checklists. We were in trouble.

Or so we thought.

As it turned out, our meeting went off without a hitch, and Sue said something so profound when we told her about our worry over the state of our house: "What matters for a child is not the things they have, but rather the love they feel."

She is so right! That is the most important gift a child ever receives—love.

As I read the letters upon letters that came in for *Mother's Message in a Bottle* that was the message I kept reading—love.

I've had the great opportunity to watch the love that my wife invests in our girls on a daily basis and through the challenges, drama, and frustration. It occurs to me that no matter what, the most important message that moms deliver is underscored by—love.

Please enjoy this book that love wrote. I extend a warm thank you to all the moms who joined us and shared their messages of love, leadership, and legacy so that all of us may learn and be inspired.

Before you give this book to your child or children, take a few moments and write them a letter, even a few words, in the blank pages we have left for you at the end of the book. There is never a bad time to tell your children how important they are to you, and when you do, you will open doors of opportunity for them and the generations to follow.

Your Part

In this book we some great moms have graced our pages with their messages of hope, love, and inspiration to their children. Their hope is to leave a legacy with their children through their words and caring. Our hope is that their words and caring can help you to leave a legacy with your children.

Before you give this book to your child or children, take a few moments and write them a letter, even a few words, in the blank pages we have left for you. There is never a bad time to tell your children how important they are to you, and when you do, you will open doors of opportunity for them and the generations to follow.

Mothers's Message in a Bottle is meant to be as much a resource about love and caring from other mothers as it is to be one from you. A letter from you will mean so much to your kids. So, we have given you priority seating as the first letter in the book. This will ensure that your letter takes its rightful place as the first thing that your children will read.

To help you write your letter, here are some tips. Sit back and relax. Take some time for yourself and just think about your children. Ponder this question: "If I had twenty minutes of my child's time, what one thing would I want them to remember forever and pass on to their kids?" Take a few moments to jot down some thoughts. Organize those thoughts into a letter. You may wish to begin with a rough draft.

Write from your heart and be as authentic as you can—the love and passion you convey in your letter will mean so much to your children and their children's children.

Loving Letters for Life

Proud Yet More Humble of the Gift of Each of You

Dear Mark, Beth, and Katherine,

When you find this message, washed up on the shore of some busy day, it will be another way to articulate my love, respect, joy, and blessing to you, our three wonderful children.

I trust this love and respect has been continually modelled and articulated for you through the years. Perhaps this one more form of "message" will help cement in perpetuity the reality of love for each of you. I trust this message will do just that!

You are well into the reality of your own children "leaving the nest." College years, professional education, marriages, and their busy lives enhance your lives and magnify your dreams for them into the experiential reality of children raised with love, goals, discipline, and faith.

You have taken the values that your dad and I have valued and built into your lives and transferred them so masterfully with the Master's help to your very own children. This we watch with awe and respect, knowing that these values will be passed to the next and the next generation.

We have taken the best from the loving homes we came from to pass on to you.

The basis of our values is spiritual in depth and dimension.

... We believe that God created us to reflect His glory, and His value of life and lives that intersect daily with our lives.

1

. . . We believe in hard work and in focused directives that enhance our lives and the lives of others.

. . . We believe in including the discipline and appreciation of education, the arts, the professions, and a free society to uphold and protect.

. . . We believe in trans-generational respect, appreciation, and care for all ages, all stages of life so gloriously given to us.

. . . We believe in relationships that enhance and bring joy and health to us, and to society as a whole.

. . . We believe in fun as well as work, travel for understanding and enjoyment, reading to enhance learning and the pleasure of words formed to create pictures of life.

. . . We believe in the union of one man and one woman to adore each other, to procreate to bless the world, and to bless generations to come.

. . . We believe in education as an ongoing life mandate.

. . . We believe in serving and giving to others through our work as the highest of callings.

. . . We believe in a personal relationship with our Lord, praise and worship of His name.

And…we believe in you.

We believe that you are responsible, delightful, educated, charismatic adults who are making a huge impact on a hurting world.

We could not be more proud and yet more humble of the "gift" of each of you, Mark James, Beth Naomi, and Katherine Ellen.

Love,

Your mother

Naomi Ellenborg Reed Rhode, CSP, CPAE Speaker Hall of Fame has been a global force in speaking, authorship, and the ministries. She is a wonderful mother whose warmth, enthusiasm and unique insight help her to create powerful and meaningful relationships. She is the author of three inspirational books, The Gift of Family, More Beautiful than Diamonds, *and* My Father's Hand. *Find out more about Naomi at www.naomirhode.com.*

Love Fully Each Day of Your Life

Dear Jenna,

I loved you before you were born. I always thought that one could never know the depth of their mother's love or love someone as much as a mother can, until they became a mother. But every day when I hug you and you decide how you will return my love—through a hug or kiss or by telling me that your heart bursts with love for me—you have shown that this is not necessarily so. You love me just as fiercely as I love you, and that gives me the best feeling in the whole world. I never knew how powerful the love and bond between a mother and daughter could be. My life with you is absolutely priceless, and you are so very precious to me. I treasure each moment we spend together. I am so lucky you are my little girl, and I look forward to each new day with you.

One of my favourite experiences with you was your first trip to Walt Disney World in August 2011. You learned about this vacation on your birthday, almost three months before the trip. You counted down the days so patiently on your calendar. What a joy the trip was! It was your first airplane ride, and you took it all in stride. You waited so calmly for every ride and character greeting at Disney World. I didn't know you could do that! I am very proud of you.

The best part of the trip was about you and the princesses. In the Magic Kingdom, you went to the Bibbidi Bobbidi Boutique. My little princess was transformed before my eyes into Cinderella, your favourite princess. You soaked up every moment while picking out your costume, nail polish, comb, and makeup. The dressing room was elegant, and it was magical as you looked at your beautiful dress. Watching you have your hair, nails, and makeup done was delightful as you enjoyed every second and entertained your own Fairy Godmother in training. Then, the most magical moment came when you were turned around to see yourself in the mirror for the first time. That smile and happiness were priceless. I will never forget it!

Afterwards, it was off to lunch with Cinderella. It was the first time you had met her at Walt Disney World. It was a dream come true for you. You loved her and chatted up a storm. She loved you right back. In fact, you made many visits with Cinderella during our trip. Watching you with Cinderella was another time I won't forget. You were just thrilled and had such wonderful conservations. She gave you so many hugs and even told you a secret, which you have always kept.

There were so many wonderful experiences for you on our vacation. From dancing and singing with Princess Aurora to the special time you had with Belle. You were proclaimed a real princess and received your own tiara and glass slipper engraved with your name, the date, and a special message—"when you wish upon a star."

Jenna, I always want you to continue to make your wishes and pursue your dreams! You deserve every happiness. You are a wonderful daughter, and I am so thankful you are my little girl. You make my life magical and I wouldn't change a thing. I know sometimes I don't always give you what you want and life might be tough at times, but I always love you no matter what for the rest of my life and beyond. I will always be there for you through the good and bad. I want nothing but a wonderful life for you. Work hard, play hard, be true to yourself, and love with your whole heart. I love you, Jenna—always and forever no matter what!

Love,

Mommy

Wendy Tarrel's most important job is being a loving mother to her beautiful daughter Jenna who at time of publication was five years old. During the day Wendy can be found at her other job as a passionate marketing instructor at a community college.

Recovered to a Better Place

Dear Hunter and Becca,

I am writing you today with more love than I ever could have imagined possible. You are two and a half years old and thirteen months old as I write this letter. In such a short period of time, you have helped me understand the word "unconditional" and you have reminded me how to live in the present. Today you inspire me to stay sober, to be grateful for all that I have been blessed with, and to make the most of each day I am given. You make me happier than anything else in the world could ever do.

As a recovered alcoholic I can share with you that these feelings were once foreign to me. In the depths of my disease I was challenged to understand what true love was. My actions were driven by selfishness and fear consumed me. Thankfully I found another way of living and, through that, a life that I couldn't have hoped for in my wildest dreams. In fact, if I was asked ten years ago to describe the life I wanted, I would have cheated myself as I would not have been able to imagine all the treasures that life could hold for me. The gifts I have received are truly unbelievable and, through sobriety, the stars have aligned beautifully. The challenge for me is to never lose sight of this.

I want you to know, however, that my sobriety is a gift that I cherish one day at a time. With each challenge life presents, an alcoholic is challenged to stay sober and to handle that situation and all the emotions it brings about. Sometimes it's tempting to escape…to run away from the feelings. I pray to God that I never again think that my only solution is to pick up a drink to escape, but if I ever end up there, I want you to know these things:

~ I love you more than words can describe and my turning to alcohol is in no way a reflection of you or your actions. The decision to pick up a drink and to not deal with the challenges life has presented to me is mine to own, not yours.

~ I never wanted to disappoint you or let you down. I want to be the mother you can count on for everything…cheering for you at soccer games, helping you with homework, and creating the most magical holidays.

~ I wanted to give you everything you ever needed or wanted, be it a trip to Walt Disney World, a new puppy, or a flashy sports car… most of all, a loving home where you feel safe, supported, loved, and cherished.

~ I always wanted to be there for you in times of need…if you're struggling in school, if you're having a hard time with your friends, or even when you're making decisions about your future. Know that I am always in your corner, even when I am not physically by your side.

~ I never meant to cause you shame or embarrassment. I want you to be proud of me and to be a woman you look up to…God willing, maybe even an inspiration.

~ I wanted to bring you laughter and joy, never sadness or hurt. I want to be the sunshine in your life, the person you turn to for help and smiles, someone to have fun with, and a shoulder to cry on in times of need.

~ No matter how easy you think it should be for me to quit drinking, no matter how much "sense" it makes, it is an incredibly difficult thing to do. And if I can't stop, it's not because alcohol is more important than you. It couldn't touch the value that you bring to this world and to my life. But the disease of alcoholism is incredibly complex and can overpower even my strongest feelings and desires.

If ever these things come to pass, please know that I have tried my best. Know that my actions do not reflect how I truly feel when I am healthy and am not consumed by my disease. Today I have been sober for eight years, nine months, and twenty-two days and I can tell you with absolute confidence and certainty that you are the best things that have ever happened to me. You melt my heart when you smile, when you say "stay with me" at bedtime, and when you giggle as I tickle your bellies. These are the "escapes" that I enjoy today…totally safe, totally healthy, and totally a blessing. I can't imagine my life without you in it, and I pray to God that I never, for any reason, have to experience that.

There are things that I need to do each and every day to stay sober and to be the best mom I can be to you. I pray that I can continue doing these things…not for me, but for you. Because you are two incredible miracles that have been entrusted to me and you deserve the best life has to offer. You brighten my every day and every hour. You make my life worth living…and living sober.

God bless you both,

Your sober, proud, grateful mother, Lori

Lori Barker is one of the strongest moms in the world. She has overcome some of the greatest adversities in life and today balances being a mom and helping to cure cancer as the executive director of a division of the Canadian Cancer Society.

Learning to Lead from My Heart

To my daughter and stepsons,

I may be an expert in leadership in my professional life, but I have learned to lead from my heart through my family.

Being a mom to my daughter Courtney and a stepmom to Tyler and Jordan has given me countless gifts and growth. I once went to a psychic who told me that having children in my life was crucial to my ability to be a loving person.

When Tyler and Jordan were little, I came into their lives. Tyler was four and Jordan was two. It's not easy for children to go through the pain of their parents' divorce, and I felt honoured to be allowed into their lives and to be a support person to them—they already had a wonderful mother and I was their wing person.

My memories of going to hockey games, making birthday cakes shaped like Ninja Turtles, and hugging away tears will always be etched in my heart. The fact that both boys have grown into loving and caring young men means so much.

I learned selflessness, presence, and fun from my stepsons. When my daughter Courtney came along six years later it was as if my soul recognized who I was waiting for! She was this beautiful seven-pound fourteen-ounce baby who was born with her fist in her mouth!

Courtney is my light, a beautiful person inside and out. I sang a song to her from birth that is very close to the well-known 1995 Robert Munsch line, "I'll love you forever, I'll like you for always, as long as I am living, my baby you'll be."

My wish for Courtney is that she follows her heart, loves herself first, and contributes to the betterment of the planet. My wish for Tyler and Jordan is that they find work they love, that they trust their value, and they focus on the positive that life brings.

I was/am a working mom and I travelled for my work throughout the young lives of my kids. I hope what I taught them was that you must do what you love, that you can work and be a great parent, and quality time together is the most important thing for families.

I am the person I am today because of being a mom and a stepmom. All three of the kids are adults now and yet they never stop teaching me about acceptance, life, and love.

The challenges of having children seem small now that the kids are adults. When I think of the times I drove all three of the kids home from parties because we wanted to make sure they were safe. When I think of the nights when I couldn't go to sleep until the kids returned home. It all seems a distant memory now. The funny part is that you never stop worrying even when they are grown!

I am so proud that Courtney is not a typical Gen Y—I talk to audiences about how Gen Y's live at home forever, etc. Courtney is twenty-three and lives on her own, works part-time, and goes to college. She is hard-working, caring, and responsible. Tyler and Jordan have made their way as well and, no pressure, but we are excited to be grandparents as the next phase.

Being a parent is rewarding on so many levels, but to me the most rewarding part has come now that we are adults and get to share a whole new level of connection and love.

Mom

Cheryl Cran is an internationally acclaimed writer, professional speaker, and mom. She is an expert in leadership, change, and business solutions and has been featured in Forbes Magazine, *the* Globe and Mail, *and the* Financial Post. *Cheryl is the author of four books and can be found online at www.cherylcran.com.*

Your Journey

Dear Chelsea and Foley,

I am writing this shortly after you announced that you are both going to be producing grandchildren in the next six months. And not only that, there is a set of twins. So I am going to be a grandma to three wonderful babies this summer.

I find my mind wandering to the early days, when you two were babies. They always say that becoming a mom changes your life, and it does. But, for me, it was one of the simplest and most natural changes in my life. Chelsea was born, I was a mom and from the very first second I could never remember being anything else. Being a mom, raising the two of you to adulthood has been the most enriching experience of my life.

So many memories. Chelsea, you were so tiny I could hold you along one arm. You curled up and were so easy to hold. Then Foley, you never stayed still. I could hold the core of your body but your arms and legs reached and wiggled and jiggled.

Chelsea, you were a visual infant, wanting to see everything with your large and expressive eyes. Foley, you fussed until you could walk. And walk early you did, crawling at four months, walking at eight months and running and climbing by nine months. I quickly learned that each of my children was a distinct individual.

And so it continued and continues today. I believe that a healthy sense of curiosity is important for a parent and not something we talk about. But, I was curious about how you would each view the world and it has been a fascinating journey watching you each tackle every new development in your unique ways.

The first thing I would wish for you, as you raise the next generation of children, is that your transition to parenthood is as magical and seamless as it was for me. That through the good times and the tough times, the fun times and the challenging times, you will never look back and question your decision to have children.

My memories of you and my realities today of being a mom are rich with love and laughter. I have enjoyed each and every stage of your life and development. Yes, even the teen years.

Watching you grow up and each become the strong, independent, and capable people you are today has been miraculous. I have been fascinated by the choices you have made. You both have taken some of the attributes of each of your parents, incorporated the realities of the times, and added your particular interests and strengths. The result is the interesting and successful adults you are.

My other source of joy is the close relationship you have with each other. From the day that fourteen-month-old Chelsea met her little brother to today, you have been best friends. Your partners have been included in this exclusive friendship circle, and I love to watch the four of you together. You are each unique individuals and in many ways different as night and day, but you make room for each other, respect each other, and care about each other.

I am certain that your children, the three cousins, will also be good friends.

As the next stage of the journey begins, you becoming parents and me becoming a grandmother, I know that the joy and fulfillment will only increase.

Love,

Mom

Kathy Lynn is a fantastic mom and the bestselling author of two parenting books. She also is a parenting columnist for community papers and Today's Parent magazine. Kathy truly is Canada's leading speaker on parenting issues today. Visit her website at www.parentingtoday.ca.

Until We Meet Again

Dear little Miss Erin,

I am writing a letter to you which is going to be part of a collection of letters to children from their moms in a book series by a friend of mine, Tyler Hayden. A letter to you, my sweet girl, to share what you have only been able to experience from a distance. Yet, it is a certainty in your mama's heart that you have been part of it all along and forever and always will be.

You were your mama's first baby and arrived at my side on Saturday, June 3, 1978 at 8:08 P.M. A beautiful blonde, blue-eyed girl who loved to snuggle from the get-go. Being my first baby, you were my big test at being a mom and a parent. I had stepped into a world I did not know with much anticipation and joy, while also experiencing the fears that come along with that: the fears of properly bathing you, feeding you, nurturing, guiding, and loving you. It did not take long, though, to realize it was not a job of the brain, it was one of instinct and heart.

Then on Thursday, December 6, 1984, at 2:11 p.m., you left your mama's side, through no fault of your own, and I was devastated. Looking back, I have come to learn that the day you left this earth created those same feelings I had when you were born. I had been forced to, once again, step into a brand new world and life. Not with anticipation and joy this time, but with fear and dread. I had to learn to let you go, continue my life without you physically by my side, and recreate myself and my life. I did not know how to do that, it was not anything I had been prepared for or ever could have been. I ended up realizing the same thing as when you were born though. This journey of pain and hurt I was thrown into was not a brain job either. It, too, was one of instinct and heart.

There was a time, so very long ago, and it lasted many years, when I could never see myself living a life of joy without you. Nor did I believe I would ever experience happiness again. However, over time and after much work, I came to recognize that the joy you brought me when we were together was a gift you left upon your departure. It did not go with you. It was and remains one of my greatest life gifts from you. Just as you were and still are for me, my darling girl. You have been one of my greatest achievements and I want you to know I have come to learn that your birth, life, and death were designed to serve the purpose of having your mama discover her own life's purpose.

Did I ever tell you that I knew you were a "gift" loaned to me as soon as I saw you in that first moment when you were at my side? I recall clearly a good friend coming to visit us in the hospital, shortly after your birth. She looked at you, looked at me, and said, "She is so beautiful, Debbie, beautiful Little Miss Erin," to which your mama immediately said, "She is a gift from God, for me to have for as long as He deems necessary." As our time progressed over the six short years we were together, you and I had many occasions where that message rang so true. Do you remember when I would ask you what you were going to be when you grew up? You would always shrug your little shoulders, look up at me, smile and answer me with something like, "You know, Mommy, we don't have to think about that." That would scare me so much, but I would not let you see how scared I was. I just kept pushing away those thoughts I had of not ever being able to see you grow up and continued to embrace, enjoy, and cherish every moment we had. And when everything ended on that cold December day, I was and still am so very glad we had done so. I still miss my dancing and singing partner. We had so much fun together! You were always ahead of your time: loving, kind, very much a free spirit, and a peacemaker by nature. I want you to know that even though you were only six years old when your job was done, the life you had was crammed with so much more than is usual for that age. You taught me so very much. I just wish you hadn't finished your job here as quickly as you did.

Your leaving started my devastation, and your returning to me some years later with a clear and concise message redirected my painful journey onto a path that eventually brought me to my destination of joy and happiness, once again. The message came to me out of the blue, the one and only time I have heard your voice since your leaving, as I have never dreamed of you. The miraculous message remains a huge gift you have afforded your mama, even in your absence, which is really what made it so powerful: the message that you did not feel any pain. It was a comfort for me to learn that directly from you, as I had always been so discomforted by the thoughts of what you perhaps felt that day at a time when we were not together and I had no opportunity to do that thing we both loved so very much—when your mama would hold you, hug you, and reassure you that everything would be okay and that you were safe in my arms.

I want you to know I have felt your presence many times since we've been parted. I know when you are here. I know you are, every day, still by my side as we reach out and work with lots of other people from around the world who have also had to be separated from their babies far too early. Your contribution to the world lives on and will continue to do so, even after we are together again. We will meet again. I know you are as certain of that as I am, and we will pick up our singing, our dancing, our hugs, and our loving each other where we left off, and it will feel as though this space that is now between us never existed. I know you are waiting for me and that brings me to another one of the greatest gifts you have given your mama: you have made dying easy for me.

You are loved, missed, cherished, and treasured—forever and always—and I have loved writing this letter to you, my sweet one. Love always,

~ *Mommy* ~ *xoxo*

Deborah Anthony is the author and publisher of Recapturing the Joy: A Journal for Bereaved Parents. *She wrote the book in 2006 as a result of losing her child and since then has helped parents recapture their joy though her book and TV series.*

To My Angel

My dearest Mckenzie,

*I*f I could leave you with a few words of wisdom and guidance to help you navigate your way through the long life you have in front of you it would be this. Always remember that you are beautiful in so many ways, both on the inside and the outside. You are strong and funny and sweet and kind. You are strong-willed and independent and can do anything you put your mind to or your heart desires. You have an incredible imagination and a wonderful sense of creativity. Always know and believe these things about yourself as you will be faced with many obstacles along your journey through life, but remembering these key things that make you who you are will keep you going. I believe all these things about you and you should, too. You are my biggest blessing, my best friend, my cuddle bug, and my monkey, and I will love you always and forever.

Love,

Mommy

Shannon Royce is the sales manager for the Nantahala Outdoor Center in North Carolina. She is an avid outdoor enthusiast and most importantly a loving mother to her beautiful daughter.

People Need People

My dear Amy and Greg,

I have learned a simple truth in life. People are important. Let me emphasize that. People. Are. Important. I am listing some of the things that I have learned. Few, if any, of them will be things that I have not said to you before. I am still working on them myself, and I am much older than you, so be patient. It takes time to develop these qualities, but they are well worth it and you will be better people for it.

Your dad and I have been married for over forty years. I can still name almost every person who attended our wedding and what they gave us. I have a wedding book to help me with the ones I sometimes forget. I have pictures. If you are invited to a wedding, attend the wedding, send a card, send a gift, do something. People remember. It's a huge occasion, an important celebration. Do not let it pass without some way of letting them know that you rejoice with them.

I will never forget the people who were at my dad's funeral. In my mind, I can see the whole thing clearly. I remember who called, sent a card, emailed, texted, posted condolences on Facebook. Attend the funeral, drop by for the visitation, send flowers, food, or a card. Pick up the phone. Even more than weddings, people remember who attended a funeral. Many times I have heard people remark on someone's attendance decades later. The death of a loved one is devastating. Let them know you care.

Even though I was a little out of it after your births, especially Amy's, I remember everyone who was there. Family gathered around. The people at work came in festive groups. People brought plants. I still have a baby bootie plant holder that someone gave me when Greg was born. The plant died a long time ago, but I kept that memento. Acknowledge the birth of child. There is no greater joy in a parent's life than their child.

I don't care how old I get, I still love birthdays. Shower me with attention and I might forget my age. Give me cake and ice cream. Give me presents! Give me silly cards. Take me out to eat. I am not the only one who loves that. Your birthday is an acknowledgement of your life. Your life. Don't let anyone tell you it doesn't matter. It does.

Stay in touch: visit, call, email, text, Facetime. We have so many ways to communicate and so few excuses for not doing so. Nothing is sadder than looking back with regret on lost time for what you did not do. Time is ruthless and it will not rewind or stop for you. It just keeps marching on. Use it wisely and thoughtfully. The smallest acknowledgement that you are thinking about someone means the world to them. Don't let people slip out of your life from carelessness.

Never expect to change anyone. Love them for who they are or in spite of it. Encourage them to be more. You can only change yourself so be the best you can be for them. If you can't work it out, walk away. Not everyone is meant to be in your life, but you can till pray for them and love them. God, in His wisdom, will put the right people in their life. It may not be you. Accept it.

I am not perfect. Neither are you. I know this is a great shock. Learn to forgive and forget. It's hard. I have held hurt inside me for years. You know what it does? It destroys you. Is it hard to forgive? You bet it is. It's even harder to put it so far in your rear-view mirror that you forget it even happened. Learn to do it. It's a skill worth acquiring. Remember the "do unto others" rule. Do you want people to forgive your mistakes? Your callous remarks? Your omissions? Learn to be forgiving.

I have been mistreated many times in my life. So have most people. It hurts. It destroys your self-esteem. I have been fortunate in that, for some of those times, I have had a champion who stood up for me and comforted me. Don't let an injustice happen in front of you and walk away. It may not make you popular, but don't leave someone in pain when you can help. Be a champion.

Pay attention to people. We all drop hints about what we want, what we need. If you listen, you will notice. So many times we are disappointed that someone was not paying attention—some people to the point of suicide. Maybe it is you who needs someone paying attention. Listen. Pay attention. And when you get the message, act on it.

I cannot tell you how much a simple smile or hello or other act of courtesy or kindness has made me feel good. More than that, it has turned my whole day around. Sadly, this is becoming a lost art. Speak to people. Hold the door for someone. Offer your help to the person who cannot reach something. Be a nice person.

Do you know who I share my deepest, darkest secrets with? Do you know who I share my greatest joys with? People I can trust. Everyone needs people they can talk to without judgment or disapproval. We don't always need advice, we just need a shoulder. Also, I cannot think of a bigger disappointment than being truly excited about something, sharing it with someone, and having them dismiss it as unimportant. We need someone we know will guard our fragile moments and rejoice with us. Be trustworthy.

Give the people you love 100 percent. Life is not a fifty-fifty proposition. Don't fall for that. You have to be willing to shell out 100 percent or your chance of failing at that relationship—family, friend, spouse, whomever—greatly increases. Set the example and maybe they will give more in return.

I know there is so much that I am forgetting, but basically, I want you to be a good person. Be a loving, caring person who anyone would be proud to call friend. It was famously said that no man is an island. It is true. Neither are you. Cultivate good qualities in yourself and when you need someone they will be there for you.

I am sorry I have not always followed my own advice, but I hope you know that I love you anyway. I hope you will become people that I would like to be. I know you have the potential. All you have to do is reach out to God. He will guide your every step. And always remember that you are my sunshine!

All my love always,

Momma

Debbie Acklin is a successful writer of creative non-fiction from Alabama. She has had the privilege of travelling extensively and having many cherished adventures with her family. The greatest adventure has been raising two wonderful children!

A Unique Kind of Love

To my lovely stepdaughter Tamara,

A stepmother's love is unique beyond all measure....I didn't birth you, feed you as a baby, or watch those first steps as you journeyed out to see all the world had to offer you. I didn't nurse you or listen to your first words, play patty cake and peekaboo with you. Yet somewhere along the way, we came into each other's lives and found a way to make it work!

There were times when we didn't see eye to eye, especially in those teenage years, when I represented all you hated in life—not just an adult, not just a parental figure, and a "fake" one at that, but also your main competition for your dad's love! Oh those battles were legendary! But even though they made me cry then, I remember them with a smile today, because through those events we came to love and respect each other.

I remember so well the first day I met you. I hoped we could forge a relationship but was worried that we'd never gel, never be on the same wavelength. I loved your dad and I chose him, not you. You were just a freebie that came along with the package. But I knew even then that you were the other half of your dad's heart, and I had to make it work.

I know you were less than thrilled when I became your "step-monster" and there were things said on both sides I'm sure we both wish we could take back now, but the strange thing is that all that we've been through over the years has reinforced how I feel about you, how much I love you, and how I respect the woman you have become.

Often through the tears I thought you'd never speak another word to me as soon as you were grown, so it makes my heart swell when you call just to chat with me, not your dad, because you want to share something you figure only I could appreciate. I feel warm and so happy when you respect my knowledge and experience enough to ask for my advice and actually listen to the thoughts I share with you!

You are grown now and a mother—and somehow, amazingly, a "step" too! And as I've watched you become the woman you are today, I marvel, and I pray for your continued success. Because you have learned all I could teach you and turned those lessons into something far exceeding anything I could have done! You are a terrific mother and an amazing woman. You chose a career and motherhood, and have excelled at both. I couldn't be prouder! I hope that my example of how a woman can make her way in the world, excel at a career while still having a family, was some inspiration to you.

If I have one piece of advice to give you that I haven't voiced in the past, it is to find out what works for you and stick to it, regardless of what others tell you. You will make mistakes—as a mom, in your career, in your marriage—but as long as you follow what you truly believe to be right, everything will turn out all right, eventually! For your children, just do your best to do what they need, not always what they want. In your career, you are bright and smart and ambitious; you'll know what to do in those tricky circumstances. With your husband, make sure he always makes you laugh. So the key to my success, and yours too, I think, is to believe in yourself, don't be too hard on yourself, and remember to have fun!

I may not ever have been a mother, but you've made me a mom! And you gave me a beautiful gift of a wonderful little person who makes my heart burst when he calls me grandma! I could not possibly love you more than I do. Thanks for being my kid!

Love,

Pat

Pat Kimpton is the best "step-monster" a person could ask for—loving, caring, and supportive. In her business life she is a highly acclaimed project manager from Florida holding a PMP, Six Sigma Green Belt, and is an emeritus board member with PMI Tampa.

I Love You Because ...

To my dear child,

When you were born, people around me began to grieve. They told me they were sorry about your problems, about the struggles you would have through life. They were sorry about the different life I would have because you were not the child they expected.

I, however, was thrilled to meet you. I loved you because I knew you would encourage me to be the best parent I could be. I loved you because you would force me to notice all the little steps it takes to master "the simple things" in life. I loved you because you would help others realize how special life is. You would show the world that life comes with varying strengths and struggles in all of us.

I have watched as you took in the world through your ears and eyes first. You always showed immense joy at the wonders in front of you. As you began to learn how your hands, arms, and legs worked, you opened my eyes to all the secrets of our world, sometimes as I rushed to protect you from your own curiosity. As you found your voice, I felt surrounded by the melody of your sounds. Your use of sounds became a symphony celebrating the life you were living.

As you have grown, you have taught me to love you because of the courage you have shown when faced with physical challenges. You have taught me to understand the intricacies of the human body and how many things can go wrong but can be "fixed." You have not let your body or mind stop you. You have always challenged us to help you go further.

I love you for what you have taught me about "school learning." You helped me understand how much is assumed to be in place when a child starts school. You have been a teacher to your teachers, showing them how many parts of development and learning have to be taught. You have helped them understand the meaning of the word "assume" and to no longer do that when working with you and other children who learn differently.

I have been excited to see you become a friend to other children in your world. You never noticed their "differences." Rather, you felt that everyone was perfect, just the way they were. You have been a great role model for adults who first looked at what was wrong before considering what was okay about others.

I love you because you have taught me about how human beings develop. You have shown me how complex each developmental milestone is, and why it is important to celebrate each step along the way. Life doesn't get mastered all at once, but with each day we get closer and so do you.

I love you because you have shared with me the joys and sorrows of dealing with other people each day. You have shown me about ignorance, bias, and the inequalities of life. You have helped me to become an advocate for the rights of you and others. You have not let me give up because of the naysayers. Your smile reminded me that you were more than the sum of your diagnoses.

I love you because you helped me see the people who also love without bias, without grief, without regrets. We have shared many important moments celebrating life with them. They have shared that you have made life more special for them.

I love you because you have attitude. This has shown me that struggles don't diminish a person's ability to have an opinion, belief systems, and a desire to be independent, even as he needs to be interdependent. You have helped me believe in miracles. You have helped me come to see the greatness of human potential.

I love you because you gave me a life I would never have known to choose. A life outside of my comfort zone. A life where I am forced to notice each moment of each day in order to celebrate "the simple things" that others miss. A life where I am required to think of someone else other than myself. A life where I have to be creative in order to get from one place to another. You have expanded my skills and for that I am grateful.

I love you because you have loved me, despite my faults, flaws, and imperfections. You have allowed me to understand that we all have a higher purpose in life. We simply need to be open to accepting the challenge and blessing.

I thank God every day that he allowed me to be your parent. I pray that we have many more adventures together as you grow and reach for your full potential.

Love,

Mom

Pat McGuire MD, FAAP is a professional speaker, author, and certified developmental and behavioural pediatrician who has worked with hundreds of families providing diagnostic and counselling and support services. She is the author of the award-winning book, Never Assume: Getting to Know Children Before Labeling Them. *Visit her at www.allchildrenarespecial.com.*

I Don't Know How to Begin

Dear kids,

I don't know how to begin
to take all my feelings, thoughts, and memories of you
and permanently encase them in ink

Memories flow in and out
like water lapping at beach's edge after the motor boat has passed
Gentle, slowly easing
until the next surge passes through

The days of your births
I knew of your differences from the beginning
Kaethen: slow, quiet, silently observing.
Colin: faster, harder, roaring into the world.
And now
"Kate, keep it down."
"Colin, does he ever speak?"
No, she won't; yes, he does
Each of my children, so much of you, so much of me

Years spent apart
strings of love binding us together
neither time nor distance could separate us

Remembering.
Days together.
Endless afternoons at the cottage
laughter tumbling from your curly-haired heads. Easy. Joyous.
Colin's red long john PJs and rubber boots,
Kate's books piled high in every room,
moments etched in my mind for an eternity.

Remembering.
Too many days that have slipped by unaccounted.
Unobserved.
Separate.
Homework in the kitchen.
Bad dream fears.
Firsts...hockey games won, school awards, kisses,
pieces of your lives shared in our irregular car rides,
watching, listening, yearning to learn every scrap of your lives in our
    brief moments together.

Kaethen. Kate, now.

My best friend.
Brave enough to face your challenges
and stand firm in who you are,
what you love.
I will always stand by you.

Colin.
Married to his best friend.
This fine young man
will always be my
son.
The one I left behind but never apart.

Celebrating
Each joyful event I was blessed to share

Imagining
Every dream that you have coming true

Believing
In both of you

I didn't know how to begin
To open my feelings, thoughts, and my life
and permanently encase myself in you.
Now, I don't know how to begin
to imagine anything else.

Thank you, my beautiful children, for inviting me into your lives.

~ Momma

Sharon Skaling is a wardrobe lifesaver who will help you find the "total you." She provides consulting and training for image and business etiquette. She is a loving mom who has stood beside her children, ensuring that they felt loved and supported even in the darkest of hours. Visit her at www.sharonskaling.com.

We Don't Have to Be Supermoms

To my daughters Laurie and Jennifer,

*a*s I write this letter there are so many thoughts and emotions racing through my mind that it is difficult to accurately express what I am feeling. There are no books that can truly tell us how to be a perfect mom. Every child is different with their own unique strengths. It amazes me that I have been so blessed with such caring, giving, and independent girls.

One of the most terrifying times in my life turned out to be one of the most precious moments a mother and daughter could share....One evening as I was driving home, a little boy ran across the street in front of me. I managed to slow the car down just in time to avoid seriously injuring the boy. I insisted we take him to the hospital to be thoroughly checked by a doctor. I was so scared and shaken. Your father was away at the time, so I phoned home from the hospital to tell you both what had happened. Laurie, you were in university, and Jennifer, you were still in school. To my surprise and relief, and without my prompting, you arrived by taxi at the hospital to be with me. You became the parents that evening. You both knew I needed you and you were there. I love you for that. Remember to allow your children to help you. It is sometimes faster to just do things yourself, but let them help. If you let them help with the little things they will be there for the big things.

Again I saw unconditional love and caring when I was diagnosed with breast cancer. Laurie, you came with your father and me to my first on-cologist appointment with your notebook in hand. You made sure I made the right decisions, you asked the difficult questions, and you wrote down everything the doctor said. I don't think your father and I heard much that day, but you were there and you were focused. You also came with me for my chemotherapy treatment, knowing full well you would have to watch them put the needle in my arm (many times because of small veins) and yet your phobia of needles did not stand in the way. I love you for that.

Jennifer, you could hardly wait to finish your university year in the West. When you did, home you came and spent the summer with me. You were with me when we got the good news the cancer had not spread to my bones. You included me in everything, even taking me along for the drive when you went for summer job interviews. We walked, we talked, and we had fun. I love you for that.

You both will remember our "treat days," or should I say "cheat days." It was on these days you would take a day off school, lounge in pajamas, and then go out for a special treat. You were not sick but you needed a day to rest your minds and do fun things. It was on these days we would go out for lunch at your favourite spot (chicken fillet sandwiches come to mind) and vow the Code of Secrecy that no one (especially your father) would ever know where we had lunch. I think he somehow knew when we were not hungry at suppertime and the room was filled with giggles. These days were so special to me, and I think they made you feel special, too. Teach your children that they are important because their need to be special is every child's hope.

You both have children of your own now. I knew you were ready to walk the road of Motherhood by the look of love in your eyes when they were born. The love you felt glowed from every part of your beings. You both would cuddle them close, smile as you watched them sleep, and talk that silly little language that mothers seem to master instantly. This love will carry them through good times and difficult times.

The pride you both showed presenting your little ones to me assured me you will do whatever you can to make sure your children know they can accomplish anything in life; you will give them the tools and boost their confidence whenever they need it.

I also saw the scared look in your eyes. You were taking on a whole new chapter in life. You had no previous experience in this "motherhood role." This tiny little baby in your arms was the most precious thing you could ever imagine, yet their total dependence was most terrifying. You girls who were so highly capable in all you set out to do, you knew this was a time to ask questions and not be afraid to ask for help. We don't have to be Super Moms. The declaration of independence, "I do it," that you taught us, Jen, from the time you could talk, was a very common phrase in our household. You both knew it was time for this motto to be put aside for a little while.

My advice to you is to continue to be the daughters you are. Your love shows every day through the caring you have for your family and for the children you teach each day. As teachers you both have so much to offer. You will stop at nothing to provide what is needed not only for your own children but for the children you nurture every day.

Teach your children to be proud of themselves but humble enough to know we are not experts at everything.

Don't sweat the small stuff. Children will rebel, tell lies, and constantly try our patience as they are finding their way.

Ask God for help through the difficult times.

Remember you can always come to "Mama" for help whenever you need me.

I love you both.

Mom

Margaret Andrews is a mom from a small town in Cape Breton who committed early on to giving the best life for her children though the gifts of love, caring, and time. She personifies commitment to family and caring for others even through the depths of breast cancer.

My Son

Dear Mitch,

The war was far from Saigon when I agreed to escort six babies from Vietnam to their adoptive homes in the United States. As president of the Iowa chapter of Friends of Children of Vietnam, I'd coordinated collecting and shipping five tons of supplies in three years to help the orphans there. Then they asked if I'd volunteer to bring six infants to their awaiting adoptive families. We had applied for adoption of a son through FCVN but didn't expect him for at least two years. Still, I thought it would mean something to him someday to know his mom had been to his homeland.

Although our government assured me I'd be safe, the decision to leave your dad and two toddler sisters was not easy. When the war escalated, I had knelt in church, begging God for a sign that I could back out of my commitment. But instead He filled me with a courage and confidence I could explain to no one. Somehow I knew this was all a part of God's plan.

By the time I landed in Saigon, bombs were falling outside the city! Vietnam was falling to the Communists! And I learned that President Ford had okayed Operation Babylift. Scores of the estimated fifty thousand Amerasian babies and toddlers were herded into the FCVN headquarters in preparation for the airlift.

On my third day there, over a breakfast of bread and bottled Coke, Cherie, the director said, "LeAnn, you've probably figured this out...."

I hadn't.

"You and Mark applied for adoption of a son, but you won't have to wait two years." She spoke above the din of bawling babies. "Obviously everything has changed. You'll be assigned one of the babies gathered here—or," she paused and touched my hand, "or you can go into the nursery and choose a son."

I sat stunned, speechless.

I felt myself flush with excitement—then with fear.

"Really?" I finally croaked. Surely I had heard her wrong.

Cherie's tired eyes danced. "Really."

"So I can just go in there and pick out a son?"

Cherie nodded again.

Dazed, I approached the door to the nursery. I paused and took a deep breath. It was like a fantasy. A dream come true.

I opened the door and entered a room filled with one hundred babies. Babies on blankets and mats. Babies in boxes and baskets and bassinets and cribs.

How would I ever choose?

But there you were …. wearing only a diaper, with your round tummy bulging over its rim. I watched as you pulled yourself up to stand beside a wooden crib and tugged the toes of the baby sleeping inside. Then you looked at me, dropped to your hands and knees, and began crawling to me. We met halfway across the room and I picked you up. You looked at me and smiled brightly, showing off your chubby cheeks and deep dimples. As I hugged you, you nestled your head into my shoulder.

"Maybe you'll be our son," I whispered. You pulled back, staring into my eyes, still smiling. For the next hour, I carried you around the room, looking at all the infants, touching them, talking to them. All the while, you babbled, smiled, and continued to cuddle. I couldn't bring myself to put you down as I went upstairs where the floor was carpeted with even more babies. The hallway was like a megaphone, blasting the sounds of chattering workers and crying babies.

I put you down to hold other infants, but each time you reached your chubby arms out for me. I snuggled you close and you snuggled back.

Downstairs, we meandered from mat to crib as I looked at all the babies again. I wished I could adopt them all. But I knew there were long waiting lists at the Denver headquarters of hundreds of families who had completed the tedious, time-consuming application process. Each of these precious orphans would have immediate homes carefully selected for them.

"How do I choose?" I murmured.

You answered by patting my face. I sat down on the floor, slowly rocking you back and forth in my arms. I whispered a prayer for the decision I was about to make, a decision that would affect many lives forever. You nestled into the hollow of my neck, reassuring me that the choice I was about to make was the right one. I could feel your shallow breath and tender skin as you hugged me back.

I recalled all the data we had collected for adoption, all the letters of reference from friends, bankers, employers, all the interviews with the social workers.

It had all been worth it for this moment...as awesome as childbirth.

We rocked in silence and cuddled. Then, with immense joy, I walked back through the nursery door to the office.

"Meet our son, Mitchell Thieman!" I announced, hardly believing my own words. Everyone gathered around and embraced us. I looked at your puzzled face and held you closer. Cherie brought a name tag and I eagerly scrawled on it "Reserve for Mark Thieman" and placed it on your ankle. Oh, how I wished your daddy and sisters were there.

Joyful tears streamed down my cheeks. I no longer wondered why I had been driven to make this journey. "This is why God sent me to Vietnam," I whispered.

I had been sent to choose a son.

No, you chose me.

This was God's plan. And I thank Him for it...and you...every day.

Love,

Mom

After Mitch and his sisters "flew the coop," LeAnn Thieman became a professional speaker and author, sharing lessons learned from Operation Babylift. She and her husband, Mark, who have been blissfully married for forty-three years, love life in Colorado. Visit this hall of fame speaker at www.leannthieman.com.

Try Many Things

Dear kids,

*F*or many years, I struggled with being happy, so the first thing that I wished for you was that you would be happy in your life. But I recall a conversation our rabbi had with a group of parents a year or so before your bar mitzvah. He asked all the parents what they wished for their children, and we each answered. Happy and healthy were the most frequently expressed wishes. He looked at us, and said, "What about wishing that your child grows up to be a good person?" I realized that all of us had wished for what we wanted our kids to get out of life, and not what we wanted our children to contribute.

As you know, a mitzvah (or commandment) is to do good. While I hope you will be happy and healthy and have much joy in your lives, I also hope that you find ways to make a contribution. Every one of us is different and has different things to offer. What are your secret passions, your secret gifts? How will you make someone's life better? Or make the planet a better place? Or solve some issues that need resolving?

How can one ever really know what the gifts are that we have to give? I know someone who has been struggling in his life, with feelings of hopelessness and depression. He is in a job he dislikes and doesn't know what to do about it. As with many things in his life, he took what was offered without bothering to think about what he likes or to actually search for himself. He leaves things to the last possible minute, panics, and either misses opportunities as a result or settles for something inadequate. When faced with actually having to make decisions, he waits for others to propose alternatives and then immediately notices what is wrong with each alternative. He predicts the worst and often gets it.

He has little joy and certainly does not feel as if he is contributing.

What I wish for you instead is to think about what you want, what you like, and to try out many things. Through experimenting and evaluating you will advance along the path and get to know yourself. This is how you find out what you are good at, who you want to hang out with, what your strengths are (and the stuff you suck at!).

One day when I was about eighteen, I returned home from university to visit my parents, feeling depressed and a little shell-shocked from my first months away from home. My dad took me upstairs, out of earshot from everyone and told me this. "You are the kind of person who will not accept what others say—you usually want to find out or decide for yourself. There are very few things in life that you cannot change or change your mind about. If you have a baby, you have a baby. You can't undo that. If you commit suicide, you are dead. You can't change that. But for all other things, if you have made a mistake, you can change it. So carte blanche. Go forth and do what you need to do." This was the most empowering conversation in my life.

This became known as the "Carte Blanche" speech in our family. So that is what I wish for you. Go forth and explore the world. Find out what you need to find out to have happiness and health, and learn how you can make your unique contribution.

Carte Blanche!

Shelle Rose Charvet is a powerful professional speaker and author of Words that Change Minds, *which is now published in over eleven languages. She has been featured on* CBC *and* CNBC *and has been described as "Einstein meets Lucille Ball." Check her out at www. successstrategies.com*

Believe in Yourself!

Dear kids,

*P*ersonally, I feel that one of the most difficult, rewarding, hair-pulling, and even challenging things a person can do in their life is be a parent!

I am one of those parents who likes to consider myself very open and honest when it comes to (all) my kids. I am a mother of three boys. They are five, fourteen, and eighteen, and no the youngest was not an "oops." His dad and I were so happy when Nathan arrived, healthy and, yes, another boy! Being a mom, especially to our first two sons, Mathew and Cameron, I had to deal with not just parenting, but also having epilepsy myself. The boys were AMAZING though—kids usually are in most crisis situations; they are for the most part very resilient. (I wish more adults were, too.)

In 2002 I underwent neurosurgery to try and lower my seizures. Little did I know that this surgery would free me of them. I have been 100 percent seizure-free since my surgery, and I have to say that my two sons Cameron and Mathew were a huge part of where I am today. I owe a lot to both of them for their support and understanding. They might have only been eight and four at the time of my surgery, but they were great and very, very helpful. I just had to remind Mathew that if he called 911 again to say "seizures" not "Caesars." Now that he is eighteen, he laughs at that! Through my struggle to get better, healing from the surgery and the after effects, I always tried to put my boys first. I do know I had times when they thought Mom was in her own world or just not there.

I wish at their ages they had understood where I was, but because they never gave up, I came back.

I started public speaking a year or so after my surgery, and I haven't stopped! It was my calling. I am so proud that my middle son, Cameron, now fourteen, is speaking with me. In February 2013 Cameron took the stage for the first time and spoke on what it was like for him having a mom with epilepsy. Cameron is a lot like me: stubborn, caring, always on the go, sensitive, and wanting to help others. I dealt with epilepsy almost my whole life, and now Cameron is dealing with another struggle that actually the whole family is dealing with: ADHD, Attention Deficit-Hyperactivity Disorder.

I thought my world was upside down, dealing with everything I went through. Now I am trying to help Cameron through his own glitches and also trying to show him that he can do anything he puts his mind to; he just has to stay positive. Cameron is in a boys' school for this school year and it's a place for him to hopefully get better, deal with his situation, and better understand it. Cameron said something to me a couple of months back. He had been at the school for about three months when he approached me in a conversation and said: "I want to open a school like this for kids when I am older." WOW! Instantly, I was running a zillion things through my mind, thinking, "He could do that!" and "Cameron would be an excellent mentor for others." Cameron also told me he wants me to help him get started in public speaking on the topic of ADHD. I couldn't be prouder of him for asking me to help him with that. So, I suppose Cam and I have a lot of work ahead of us, and I am truly looking forward to it!

Cameron loves to help other people. He might have some really off days but deep inside him he knows that there is always hope. I have a tattoo on the inside of my right arm that says *BELIEVE* and I look at it every day, because I do believe that things can be turned around for the better. People can forgive others and life is full of struggles sometimes; in saying that, I think people need to pick and choose battles as sometimes they really aren't that important or worth risking things over.

I sincerely hope that my three boys know where I am coming from, that I will always be there for them in any situation, and that I will always do my best to guide them all in the right direction. We all take different paths in life and that is not a bad or wrong thing, but I just want my boys to know I believe in them. And mostly I want them to believe in themselves!!

Love,

Mom xox

Ann Marie Gillie is the author of Let's Talk About Epilepsy *and* If These Walls Could Talk: Don't Let Epilepsy Control You. *She believes that great things happen in people's lives; you just need a little patience. Today she shares her experiences of having neurosurgery for her epilepsy and of living a seizure-free life. Visit her at www.anngillieepilepsyspeaker.com.*

Dear Cerebral Palsy

Dear CP,

C an I call you that? I just think we should be on a first name basis by now. You invaded my life when my youngest daughter was thirteen months old. When I first learned about your existence, I was in total "mama bear" protector mode. Googling until all hours of the night, wondering how I could "fix" this.

After a rather uncomplicated NICU stay, we really weren't expecting anything to crop up. But wow! You are definitely sneaky! If I had written this letter a year ago, I probably wouldn't have very many nice things to say to you, so you should be glad I'm writing this now. My mother taught me if I don't have anything nice to say, do not say anything at all. Be glad for that lesson.

Thank you for targeting my daughter. Sounds weird, don't you think? Don't let this go to your head or anything. I'm still not overly happy that you decided to make yourself comfortable within my family, but I do have to thank you for sending me the best teacher I have ever had. Jillian has showed me that I am MUCH stronger than I have ever given myself credit for. Speaking of strength? Jillian is one of the toughest kiddos I've ever met. And the sense of humour? I'm quite thankful that she got that from me, and we can laugh about things together.

I'm not happy with the fact that my awesome daughter gets frustrated watching other children walking and running. Or when she wants to do something like sit on a potty and she's too tight to make it happen, how she cries for me to make it better, and I can't. I really hope this lesson is learned quickly because I'm pretty sure that neither Jillian nor I enjoy it much.

Thank you for teaching BOTH of my children that "normal" comes in every shape and size and ability. Instead of my children asking me what's "wrong" with a child (or adult) they already consider that there is NOTHING wrong with them. In fact, you've taught my older daughter to be Jillian's biggest supporter. I suppose I should thank you for that as well.

As much as this has been a roller coaster with you in our lives, I should be glad that you picked on a family who will stand up for their child. I feel like I fight for everything, but to see Jillian succeed at something makes it all worthwhile. My daughter may have cerebral palsy, but it doesn't define her. You don't define THIS family. We're just muddling through the best we know how.

Sincerely,

Cheryl Peters, Jillian's fearsome mama

Cheryl is a stay-at-home mom by day, blogger by night. Blogging is a way to maintain any remaining marbles she has left. After growing up in Nova Scotia, she now calls Toronto home with two daughters, a husband, and a cat. Her personal blog is: beautifulsideofhectic.com where she mostly writes about her youngest daughter's journey with cerebral palsy.

I Count You More Than Once

My dear daughters,

Condensing a lifetime of insight and experience into a single message is an impossible task, but here are my thoughts for today.

Believe beyond all words that you are loved beyond measure. Know this in your hearts always. It's one of life's greatest pleasures to be known and loved for who you are—smiles and joys, fears and frustrations, warts and all. And I truly love you.

Pay close attention to who and how you are in this world. Character matters. The rest—the having and the doing—will follow.

Dig deep to find your values and claim your strengths. Troubles come and troubles go. When you live from a firm foundation you make strong choices and set solid directions.

As much as possible, learn how to stand on your own two feet and care for yourselves. It's not the job of others to solve your problems and pave your way. They're all dealing with their own stuff. Holding a sense of entitlement (believing the world owes you) will always leave you wanting. At the same time, don't be afraid to reach out for help, and be ready to lend a hand to others.

None of us knows how the future will unfold. In the absence of information, assume it will arrive, bringing wonder and delight. Don't borrow trouble by fretting about problems that may or may not lie ahead.

Assume life's responsibilities with enthusiasm. Start each day knowing you are blessed with countless possibilities and choosing from a candy jar of delights.

Life is a series of swings and contradictions. Maybe you have money but no time. Maybe you have big responsibilities, but very little freedom. On it goes in endless combinations. As dizzying as it may be, live with joy from wherever you may be hanging on the pendulum of the moment.

Life goes fast. Be present for today's moments, savour your memories of things past, and take pleasure in anticipating what comes next.

Live with gratitude. It lifts your spirits and spills joy to others.

Know, again, that I am ever thankful for your presence in my life. When I count my many blessings, I count you more than once.

With Love,

Mom

Patricia Katz is a fantastic mom, artist, and hall of fame speaker. She is a bestselling author and has been featured on CBC, *and in the* Globe and Mail *and* National Post. *She is a strategist for life balance and productivity and served as spokesperson for Proctor and Gamble. Pat lives a life and inspires us to "Press Pause…Think Again." Find out more about Pat at www.patkatz.com and www.pauseworks.com.*

A Mom Is Still A Mom

Dear son,

A mom is still a mom, even if she isn't the one that gave birth to you.

A mom is the one who is there for you when you need her to sew a costume, take you to the dentist, and comfort you when you have had a bad day.

A mom is the one who teaches you to wish on a star, helps you dye Easter eggs, finds those special gifts at Christmas, and makes sure you have the right number of candles on your birthday cake.

A mom is the one who cheers for you at your baseball games, takes you to swimming practice and attends all of your music recitals.

A mom is the one who makes sure you eat right, have underwear and pajamas that fit, gives you medicine when you are ill, and worries about your health.

A mom is the one who makes the rules, takes the heat as the bad guy when you think the rules are unfair, and hopes for the best when she lets you get away with breaking them on occasion.

A mom is the one who makes you clean your room, set the table, empty the dishwasher, and do other chores around the house—not because she can't do those things but because you are part of the family.

A mom is still a mom, even when you are a grown man living far away.

A son is still a son, and very much loved in every way, even if he was given birth by someone else.

Love,

Dar

Darlene Law is stepmom to Vance, wife to Alvin, and the brains behind the talent of AJL Communications, a motivational speaking business located in Calgary, Alberta. Find out more about AJL at www.alvinlaw.com.

Every Day, One Well-Lived

To my beloved daughters,

There was once a time, not so long ago, when your tiny heads rested in the palms of my hands. Now, the world rests in yours.

As teenagers, you are in a unique and short-lived position, one that, to you, seems as if it will never change. You feel that you will be in this time of teenage limbo forever, never imagining that you truly will grow up, have children, and, heaven willing, grow old. You have so little life perspective to judge or truly appreciate the place you are in today, to know that at this moment in your existence, you literally have the world available to you. Your possibilities are more limitless now than they will ever be. Strangely, many teenagers seem to feel limited and hemmed in by imagined boundaries. I think until you are truly on your own, with a family, mortgage, and full-time job, you can't really understand boundaries. My hope is that you go out there and live.

It may seem strange to get advice to live. After all, isn't that what each one of us does every day? Live? To me, living is something more than getting up each morning, attending to a list of things to do, and falling into bed exhausted at night. That is existing. Living is embracing. Living is touching, feeling, smelling, and appreciating every solitary second of your life, even if you are engaged in mundane activities such as work or school. Living is welcoming the fact that life often presents you with events and options you had not planned on or hoped for. Every experience is just that, an experience. It will teach you something you need to know. As I reflect on my life, some of the most trying situations are ones that I am now profoundly grateful for. Though often painful and unbearable at the time, I have grown and changed more through the cataclysmic than the mundane.

Want to know my secret recipe for happiness? Forgive freely. I think one of the things that we females secretly believe is that we are unique in our insecurity. I was amazed as I grew older to know that all the "popular" girls in high school (i.e., cheerleaders, drill teamers, and class officers) were just as insecure as I was. Impossible? No, true! They too worried about being viewed by others as ugly, stupid, or perhaps worse, invisible. I discovered that because they were more in the limelight, they just learned to hide their fears better. Well, guess what? That never really goes away. Sure, you grow into your skin a little, but deep down inside, I think we are all just highly functioning insecure people. Remember that. That person who did whatever unfortunate thing to you, they are tender inside, just like you. They just might hide it better. They have battle scars that are just as compelling to them as yours are to you. Forgive them. Move on. Holding on to bitterness does nothing to the person you are angry with. It affects only you. Let a lot go, be happy.

There is that saying "don't sweat the small stuff." With time and perspective, almost everything is "small stuff." Unfolding drama today most likely won't matter, or even be remembered, in a few years. Be the bigger person so that your reaction doesn't create an all new event. There is such sublime peace in the words, "It's okay. I forgive you," even if only uttered in your own mind.

As I contemplate my existence in the world, I dwell on the age of this planet, and all who have lived here before me. One person can seem very meagre indeed when you consider such vastness. These ruminations often lead toward morose feelings of how small and insignificant I am. A tiny speck in a timeless universe. Then I think about those women who lived here hundreds of years ago. I believe they had the same desires as me. They wanted to feel happy, secure, and loved. They wanted their children to feel peaceful and content with themselves. Such feelings are timeless and eternal. They are not unique to this time, this place.

Love is eternal. I can feel surges of love from those who have gone on. People I don't know and don't remember, but they are there. Many explain it away as déjà vu or just DNA. Yet, I have no doubt that it is something greater. It collects and flows around me. When your children and children's children are here and I am gone, I hope they will feel that too. Because I have a great love for them already, through you, even though they exist only in my imagination at this time.

We all just rent on this planet, yet we mean so much. We are not insignificant. Our relatively small lives can be lived in such a way to offer profound meaning to those who rent after us.

Every day, one well-lived.

All my love,

Mom

Shauna Dansie is a professional writer, editor, and storyteller who loves everything to do with words. She lives in Salt Lake City, Utah, with her husband, two daughters, and two cats named after candy bars.

Great Losses, Silver Lining

My sweet McAulay,

I have loved you since you were just an idea. You have been the most life-changing and life-affirming dream come true that any mom could dream. If I have ever questioned the path my life has taken or the purpose of anything that has happened, all I have to do is look at you and I stop questioning and understand that my purpose in this life is to be your mom. It was meant to be that your dad and I would find each other, and from that very important love would come such an amazing little man.

My hopes and dreams for you are endless, but above all those, I hope that you will have your own dreams and goals and the tenacity to chase them and make them your reality. Being a parent in the world we live in today is a challenge I couldn't have understood before we had you. It seems around every corner is lurking a potential hazard that I so wish I could protect you from. I struggle every day to balance your protection with your freedom. I want to shelter you from the negative, yet I know I have to teach you how to navigate the potential perils of the bigger world.

I sincerely regret that I couldn't shelter you from the reality of death, and losing someone you love. I am truly sorry that you had to learn from such a young age what cancer looks like in all its ugliest forms. In the cancer community, we talk a lot about "survivors," and generally the term refers to people who have survived cancer themselves. I want you to know that I also think of you as a survivor. Of course you did not survive the disease, but you have survived the loss. Having lost, between the ages of five and ten, three grandparents, I am so proud of the mature way in which you have dealt with your feelings and the way in which you choose to view the world.

From the age of three you learned what respectful behaviour is in a hospital waiting room. You were not afraid to sit with and be affectionate to your grandparents even though they no longer looked or sounded like the grandparents you knew and loved so dearly. You watched them closely at each visit to see what more cancer had taken from them. You watched all three of them eventually fade into glimpses of what they should have been. And, our hearts broke not just from our own loss, but from watching yours. At each funeral we watched our brave little man accept condolences from complete strangers as they expressed their own sadness, and in turn watched as you attempted to ease their grief with a smile or a story.

You asked questions when you were uncertain, and we were honest with you. You shed tears when you were sad, and you showed your frustration when you were angry. Sadness and anger can be very mature feelings and you have learned the hard way how to cope with the disappointment they both bring. Cancer stole from you and took something of your innocence with it. But you have not let it define you. You have such a great capacity for empathy. You have learned compassion, and there is where I find the silver lining of such great loss.

I think that compassion is such an integral part of being a good citizen of the world. You should always try to look at others and see what they can't show you. Understand that everyone has a story of their own, and you will be able to forgive them their shortcomings. I know you will be a force for good, because of your own story. Look for the needs in the world, they won't be hard to find, and do what you can to make them less. Your grandfather, my own father, was a champion of those less fortunate. He gave of his time, skills, and energy, and showed compassion to anyone in need. You will hear stories of his generosity to others and I will encourage you to model his citizenship.

I said that you are a survivor because of your loss, but never forget that your dad is a survivor because he has beaten cancer. Your dad beat his cancer before you were born, so although you have seen what it means to lose to cancer you have not gotten to witness what it is to win that battle. Cancer doesn't always win. He was so brave and so strong in the face of such a terrifying disease. He never gave in to the idea of defeat. He will forever be the very best model of the man I hope you will be.

As you get older and claim your independence, I promise to remember the things I know to be true about your character and trust you to make the best decisions for yourself. I expect that I will falter now and then, and worry myself into a frenzy. Please know that it is from the most extraordinary love that I worry, not from a lack of faith in you. I believe that at your heart, you will be a leader and not a follower. Please do not lose this confidence, it's okay to be different and to stand by your best instincts. You will always know what is right and what is wrong. Right is not always going to be the easy choice, though. I pray that you will not choose easy over right. But know this, if you do choose easy over right and find yourself in unfamiliar territory, you will never be alone. Your dad and I will always be here to help you make sense out of a bad decision, and we will not judge you by your imperfection but applaud you for asking for help. People make mistakes every day. It is what you learn from your mistakes that makes you who you are.

When I tuck you in at night (which I'll continue to do long after you think I stopped), I sometimes sit and look at you and think about how I look forward to watching you grow. Other times I wish that I could preserve you in a bubble and keep you to myself. When I dream about your future this is what I hope for you:

"Dream big and love big, you'll never go wrong. Believe in yourself, and don't lose faith in others, remember who you are. When you find that special person you are meant to share your life with I hope you experience love like your father and I have. Don't settle for less, it's worth waiting for. In life don't settle, period. Take care of your health, without it the rest is irrelevant. Remember that your mom and dad love you, and we'll always be here for you no matter what."

You are my heart, and will forever be the best I have ever done.

Love,

Mom

Heather Jones is a self-employed travel specialist who finds solutions for her clients regardless of destination. She is the caring spouse to a video game designer and the cornerstone to a very active family.

I Believe in Love at First Sight

Shelby, Olivia, Cash, and Ozzie,

When I was young and people asked me what I wanted to be when I grew up, I always answered by saying, "I want to be a mom."

I believe that my purpose in this life is to be faced with obstacles to overcome that will make me the best person I can be so that I can be the best mom to each of you.

I'm not sure that I ever believed in "love at first sight," but after giving birth to four beautiful children, I can now say without a doubt that it is real. From the first moment I looked into your eyes, and held you in my arms, I knew that no greater love could exist. The bond that formed between us the instant you came into this world is one that can never, ever be broken.

Throughout the years so far, we have been faced with many obstacles as individuals and as a family. Emotional, mental, and physical hurdles have been placed in front of us that have changed who each of us are as humans and continue to challenge us and strengthen our bodies, minds, and spirits. During these times, the one thing that has remained constant has been our love and support for each other. Even from a very young age, you have continuously surprised me with your wisdom, innocence, courage, and faith that things will be okay.

Each of you make me proud every day with your accomplishments and milestones in life, no matter how big or small they may seem. Your strength makes me stronger; your happiness makes me whole; your pain and sadness break my heart in pieces. I live my life to protect you, teach you, and guide you in the direction that I believe will lead you to the "right" path based on my experience and knowledge at the time. My hope is that you will take all of the lessons I teach you, combine them with the lessons you have learned through your own life experiences, and live the best life you can live as the best person you can be.

I have tried, but I don't think there is any way to fully capture in words all of the lessons and advice I hope to pass on to you as you grow. I will continue to work every day to ensure that you have a solid foundation of morals to help guide you through your life. You will be faced with challenges and obstacles along the way, but as long as you stay true to who you are and where you came from, I am confident you can get through anything.

Have dreams and set goals. Don't allow any bumps in the road put a stop to fulfilling what you set out to accomplish. Stay positive and surround yourself with positive people.

Trust and respect are things that have to be earned. Respect yourself, be confident in yourself, and trust yourself, and you will find that the people in your life will do the same. The only person in your life who will be there 100 percent of the time is you. You will set the standard for how people treat you by the way you treat them. Accept people's opinions, but don't let anyone make your decisions for you. If there is something you think you will regret doing, try not doing it. If there is something you will regret not doing, try doing it.

Take a stand for what you believe in. Rules are meant to be followed, but that doesn't mean they can't be changed. If you don't agree with the rules, make sure you have gathered the necessary information, and challenge them with that knowledge. If you share your opinion, be prepared to back yourself up.

Never stop asking questions. Learn something new every day. Knowledge is power and will lead you to a much more exciting and fulfilling life. Look at nature. Pay attention. Learn about the world around you.

Understand and appreciate that everyone is unique. No two people's stories are the same.

Listen when people talk. Give your friends advice when they need it. Don't spread rumours and never, ever start them. Be cautious of who you share things with. Never become completely dependent on another person. Be responsible. Admit when you are wrong.

Remember that "I'm sorry" are empty words unless your actions prove otherwise. Say "please" and "thank you." Hold the door for people.

Dance like nobody is watching and do it often. Sing like nobody can hear. Laugh a lot, and remember a smile can change anyone's day.

Stay close to your siblings. They were your first best friends, and you've shared experiences that nobody else has had. Go to family dinners. Mean it when you say, "I love you."

Read this book from front to back, and take valuable advice from all of the other amazing moms who have shared things I may have forgotten, and things I do not have the knowledge to share. I will do the same.

If you take only one thing from this letter, let it be that I love you all with my whole heart.

Love,

Mommy xoxo

Michelle is a full-time mother of two daughters and two sons living in rural Canada. Her hobbies include karaoke, checking out the latest bestsellers on her e-reader, and practising to be the next Master Chef. Her favourite things are the writing and artwork of her four children (ages eleven, six, five, and two).

Badge of Courage

Dear Brogan,

Three years ago when you were only seven, I was diagnosed with thyroid cancer. My first thoughts were of going to heaven and leaving you without a mother. I couldn't bear the thought. I started to think of all the things I had meant to do and never got around to. I had to print out all the photos I had taken and catch up on the journal I had been keeping for you. I had to write smart, witty stories in it and advice that would get you through your years. I had to figure out a way to be brave and not sad in front of you. There's a lot of pressure when you think you've run out of time. There's also a lot of regret for the things you wanted to do and didn't. Or even worse, the things you should have done and didn't when you had TIME. And then, I had to figure out what cancer I had and how to live.

We didn't tell you I had cancer because you knew from seeing it on television that Terry Fox had died of it. I never wanted you to think for a minute that I could die. When I finally told you, Aunt Jazmine and Nannie were there, crying silently behind you. You are so mature for your age, and you thought about this for some time. One day you asked me if you could "catch my cancer." That hurt me more than any needle or incision. You shouldn't have had to worry about such a thing.

After that, you proudly told people, even strangers, that "my mother has cancer." To see such confidence in a little person must have been such a surprise to them. You continue to be my brave

little soldier. When I think of how well you have handled this, I know
that your daddy's strength and calm nature made you feel secure in
all the upheaval. We are so lucky he belongs to us.

If any good can come out of having cancer, it's lessons in life. As
a police officer I have always been strong, in control, and fearless.
Suddenly nothing was in my control. It was a helpless feeling that
I wasn't used to having. Your daddy said from the start, "We have a
plan. When the plan changes, we will make a new plan." Those words
helped put everything in perspective. They helped me learn patience
and how to wait, not always silently, but with as much grace as I
could muster. I learned that I could have a say in my treatment if I
educated myself on my disease. I learned that knowledge is power,
and mightier than any badge I could carry. Doctors would listen to
me when I spoke their language.

These are the lessons I want to pass on to you. Patience, education,
assertiveness, compassion. I never thought that the biggest lessons
we would both get would come from cancer, but they have. You will
grow to be the woman you choose, but I hope that when you think
about the type of mother you saw every day, she is one you would
be proud to be like. I hope I danced enough in the kitchen for you
to know that you have to cut loose and have fun even when you feel
like crying. I hope you heard me yell at enough rude drivers to know
not to let people treat you poorly, in a car or not. I hope you saw me
cry one minute but then saw me wipe my tears the next when you
walked in the room and I asked you about your day, for it showed
you that I have vulnerability but also fortitude. I hope you saw that
it didn't embarrass me when people stared at the large scar across
my neck and that I was proud of it because it was another badge I'd
earned, this time of courage. I hope you saw the love between your
daddy and me, even through the hardest part of our lives together,
and saw how a man should treat a woman, with respect and ador-
ation. Lastly, I hope that seeing me read every day makes you hungry

for an education because you know that knowledge gives you power, and with that, anything is within your grasp.

At the age of nine, you are everything I want you to be and more. Do things that make your heart happy and your conscience clear. That's a recipe for a good life.

My sweet girl, you are the best thing I ever did and I couldn't imagine my life without you. As we say every night at bedtime...sleep well, wake happy.

Love,

Mommy

Charity Sampson is a police officer with the RCMP and resides in Ottawa with her husband, Mike, and their daughter, Brogan.

Living is a Team Sport

To my beautiful children, Keagan and Quinn,

efore I even start writing this message to you, I am crying, thinking of my life before I had you and wondering what I ever did with all that time on my hands! Now don't get me wrong, there was nothing wrong with that life. It was full of adventure and travel as I hope yours will be. However, on the day each of you were born a new adventure opened up. I became a bigger and better person because of you.

There are several things that I hope to teach you in life:

The journey is more important than the end result.

In life we all have goals. Goals are an important and necessary part of life. Reaching a goal is the best feeling in the world, as you can prove to yourself that you can follow your dreams! However important getting to the goal is, please remember that the path you take and the people you meet and the experiences you have during that journey are not to be forgotten. There are many ways to reach a goal. There are shorter ways and longer ways, easy ways and harder ways. The path that you go on is of course a choice you get to make, and you may not even know which path it is until you are knee-deep in the mud! It is that path that will define you as a person. If you reach your goals with blinders on then you will not have learned anything from the journey you just took to reach your goal. Open your eyes and your heart to all the things out there during the journey. How you deal with what you see or experience is what defines you as a person. A journey is where you learn how to take other journeys to get new results. After all, blinders are for horses, and even then I question the necessity of them!

Living is a team sport.

When you wake up in the morning you can make a decision. Try to do everything by yourself or work with others. Although it is very important to do things by yourself, you will find that two hands, two feet, one heart, and one brain can only get you so far no matter how smart you are. Open up your mind and your heart to others, and you will see that the world is endless. Many feet, many hands, many hearts, and many brains can accomplish anything in the whole world and those worlds beyond! You can't climb your first tree without a boost or run your first race without a cheerleading squad (of course that will be your dad and me) or get your first 100 percent on a spelling test without some help. You need to rely on the people who love you to help you learn and be active in your life.

Money isn't everything.

Okay, money helps with some things...but you have to realize that you can have a wonderful, full life with only the shirt on your back if that is what you want. You already know that an old egg carton makes pretty great caterpillars and that old yogourt containers make great drums. You already know that with paper, paint, and your fingers and toes you can make great works of art. Keep those things in mind before you go out to buy the new toy that you "need" or ask to go to a restaurant. Isn't it more fun to stay in and help cook a meal together?

Smiles and laughter are infectious. Mommy loves your smiles and laughs. Never stop laughing. As you get bigger you will find that there are more and more things to frown about, but don't. You will get much further along in life with a smile and a laugh than a frown and a yell. Remember that no matter what situation you are in, smile and it will all seem better!

Even if you don't learn any of these things from me, I hope you will at least learn one thing: Mom loves you both more than anything in the world. I may not be famous or have a lot of money, but I always have all the time in the world and more love than you can imagine.

Love,

Mom

Kathryn Colbert is an environmental professional living in Florida, working for the Seminole Tribe of Florida. She is the mother of two children and three dogs. She enjoys baking and going for nature walks with her children.

I Love You to the Moon and Back

Dear Piper and Sadie, (aka the Buckley Beauties),

I have tried and tried to start this letter with a little wit and whimsy, but is has proven to be harder than I thought! Not that I am at a loss for words. Rather, I'm at a loss for choosing what words to write, which pieces of advice I wish to give you, and how the heck to say it so that it will last!

There are days when I feel our worlds are going a mile a minute, but when it comes to you two, there are times when my world comes to a screeching halt. It is at these times I can't think or do anything but be in those moments that are happening right then. In times since, when I remember some of those life moments, I can actually feel the emotions all over again. Some of them make me smile just because you are my daughters, and then I laugh because there is nothing you can do about that! Like how many pictures can I take in front of the house with you dressed the same!

My advice to you is to grab your life moments, whatever they may be, and actually live in them. Don't just create a digital memory on your camera, live it, tell it, reflect on it, and smile about it.

I remember my grandmother telling my brother and me that we were pretty much her favourite Lee and Greig of all time in the history of forever. It wasn't until we had you girls that I truly understood the meaning of that sentiment. Piper and Sadie, you are pretty much my favourite girls of all time in the history of forever. I will always love you, no matter what, even if you use a Sharpie to monogram my favourite hat with your names across the beak!

Each time you two do or say something, like most parents, we are amazed, brimming with pride, and certainly entertained. Thank you! Each time you go to preschool or school, I run through my head…did I give you enough love and support to last until I see you next? Did I give you enough "street smarts" to bring you home safely? Did I give you enough encouragement to be yourselves and thrive in your days? Did I hug and kiss you? Tell you I love you? And then…okay, how long until I get to see you again?

I hope that I am doing some of the things I've aspired to inspire in you. And come to think of it, you gals are doing a bang-up job keeping me in check on this! You both have incredible and sometimes untouchable imaginations! I hope that you respect your imaginations and the power they hold. If yours is roaring with enthusiasm some day and you want to colour outside the lines, then have at it! Be proud of your choices, then rush home and tell me all about it so I can get lost in creativity with you!

Piper and Sadie, I see such genuine care and compassion for others in each of you. Even though you are only three and five years old (excuse me, three-and-a-half and five-and-a-half years old!) I truly believe you know that sometimes the smallest things in life take up the most room in our hearts. I hope you never lose this part of yourselves. These small things can be either positive or negative and can be the most substantial turning points in anyone's life.

A long time ago I overheard this advice being given: you don't have to attend every argument you are invited to but if you do accept, then argue the issue at hand, not the individual. I know it is hard to see now, but this piece of advice will help you gain clarity and proper closure on any issue. I trust in you both to be great at this!

Some of my favourite life moments with our family have happened at the beach. I love when you rush up from the water's edge to tell me about an outstanding discovery! I see your sandy toes and I wait for my salty kiss before you head back on another expedition! You both have gigantic smiles, giggles, and new-found bravery daily. I hope that you always have this as part of your lives, as it is magnificent!

I want the world for you, yet I want to shelter you from the world. Please bear with me while I work this ratio out! I want you to experience the simplest things in life since our lives can get pretty involved when we let them. I want you to touch dragonflies, catch fireflies, swim with the fish, dance with fairies, and talk to the stars and the moon. I want you to always grow up with love, patient and gracious hearts, and to always know just how much you are loved and admired.

Piper and Sadie, I love you to the moon and back.

Love always,

Mum

Lee is a wife, a mother, a bagpiper, and the creative art director for the Buckley Residence. She grew up in Pictou County, Nova Scotia, attended Acadia University, and now lives in Dartmouth, Nova Scotia, with her husband, Sean, and their two daughters.

My Message in a Bottle to the Women in My Life

To the women in my life,

I have always been the one who gets things done, and I am proud of being self-reliant. Now, in the autumn of my years, I look back and see all the things I missed because of it. We live in families so we can help each other, thus we need to learn to accept help when needed. I want you, my daughter, daughters-in-law, granddaughters, and all the women in my life, to know that life will continue going forward until the last day has arrived. If you want to live life fully, then you need to stop and smell the flowers. The flowers will not stop for you to notice them.

The first thing I would like you to know is that you are a daughter of God, and as such, a princess in his kingdom…you are, and will always be, very special.

Loving yourself will give you a full, rewarding, and happy life. Loving oneself is not being stuck-up, rude, or selfish—to the contrary, it is being loving, caring, and selfless.

Always give thanks for everything in your life, good or bad, because you will learn from the bad experiences the wisdom to become better.

Don't sweat the small stuff. If it doesn't keep you from eternal life with the God who created you, then let it pass. Otherwise, just count it as a lesson learned.

No one can make you happy. If you want to be happy—then smile and make it happen. But remember that money, selfishness, and material possessions don't give you happiness, just more things to clean…alone.

Don't ever compare yourself to anyone but you.

Never let your eyes tell you that you need something, especially when your pocket is empty.

Be frugal. In the end, you will have more than those who aren't.

Be thankful for your talents and share them often…that is how they grow.

There is a difference between being a wife and being a married woman. A wife always helps her husband to save money for a better future. A married woman is just one who lives together with a man under the law, but always does what she wants without planning for their future.

A mother finds ways daily to make time for family togetherness. She also teaches her children to play and makes sure they know how.

A mother loves her children by finding time for them when they need her: not in between chatting, playing her online games, or watching TV programs. Games, chatting, and TV programs will still be there when your children are gone—and that will happen in less than eighteen years.

On dates, your husband should be first on your list, then your children. Never neglect to spend time and show love for the father of your kids.

A wife shows love for her husband by keeping their home and clothes clean, their meals tasty and on budget. Be proud of your homemaking skills.

A wife shows respect for her husband by keeping herself clean and by wearing modest, feminine clothing.

Never speak ill about your husband after a misunderstanding. The misunderstanding will be cleared up soon enough, but the words you tell others about him in anger will be forever in their minds.

Respect yourself by taking care of your health and body; you only have one.

You don't need a man to be someone. Be the best someone there is, single or married.

Marry a man who will respect you by helping you become your best, and do the same for him.

Don't go for the easiest or fastest things in life…anything worth having is worth fighting for.

Remember that you catch more flies with honey than vinegar. Use sweet tones from the heart.

If you do these things, you will find happiness and love all the days of your lives. May you be as happy as you deserve is my hope. All my love is for you.

Love,

Mom

Anna del C. Dye is the author of clean tales of elves and romance. Visit her website for more: www.annadelc.com

If I Could Go Back

Dear Steve,

If I could go back in time, I would hug you more, kiss you longer, tickle you harder, and watch you closer. Being a teenaged single parent means you don't know much, not only about parenting but just being a grown-up. It means you are still growing while trying to raise another. And with this come many, many mistakes and huge regrets, most of which we have grown to embrace and laugh at and some we bury deep inside. But most of all, I only wish I could hold you up in my arms, squeeze you tightly and kiss your cheeks, blow fish on your belly and tickle your feet. My love for you has changed and grown into a mother's pride. You follow your dreams (even though they are not mine!), and when you smile, laugh, and dream big, I see your smiling, chubby face again. Nothing can replace those warm and happy heart smiles. I love you Steve.

Love,

Mom

Mary Teed is now a mother of one and grandma of two. Lifelong learner and lover of life!

More Lessons You Taught Me

My son Ryan,

What an amazing kid you are. When you were just three, you could already use your "I" statements. We drove you home one day from preschool and picked you up in a rush. It was late, we were hungry, and we quickly put you in the car seat and into the car and buckled you in. Partway home, we realized we fastened one of the belt buckles on the car seat but not the other. So we pulled over and quickly did the seat belt up and apologized for having forgotten.

As we continued on our drive home, we heard a little whimper from the backseat. You asked us, "Would you like me to share this at home or now in the car?"

"Now. Ryan, what is it sweetie?" we asked.

You then proceeded to share how you felt: "I'm unhappy with how unsafe that made me feel." And we realized that, yeah, we shouldn't have rushed, we shouldn't have harmed your potential safety, that you were too important to us. But the biggest lesson I took away was that a three-year-old can communicate well and even use his "I" statements.

You have done so many amazing and memorable things since then. I remember you being five and hanging out at the school gym where I taught. As a high school teacher, I spent a lot of time there coaching teens. You had twenty-four babysitters at any one time from the volleyball and basketball teams. The girls loved playing with you and you would joyfully get passed around the group. I remember solving a teenage situation after school one day while you were there. As we headed home, you commented on the tension around the poor teenager.

You asked me, "Why did that teenager do that? Why did he make that choice?"

I said, "It's because they didn't have conversations with their parents first. They only talked with their friends and made a poor choice."

Ryan, you wisely said, "Mommy, when I'm a teenager, I'll keep talking to you."

And I responded, "Can I bottle that?!"

You've taught me so many lessons. As a kinaesthetic learner, you love experiences, and touch is important to you: from playing the drums to the guitar to the piano, skateboarding or snowboarding, hockey or Lego. But the best part is when you come down in the morning after you wake up and give me a hug and say, "I love you." I love when you invite me to sit in the hot tub and have one of our stargazing hot tub chats. You are so loving and caring. I remember reflecting on my ideal clients for my business and thinking, who in my life do I love spending time with the most? Who has qualities I would like in my clients as well? Ryan, you came to the top of my mind. It is the unconditional love and acceptance you allow everyone you encounter. I built my business around working with more people like you.

More lessons you taught me:

When your dad and I raised our voices while disagreeing, you had the courage to interrupt us, because it bothered you. You didn't let us get away with this unhealthy behaviour. It's not that we were yelling, we just weren't really listening to each other. By interrupting, you reminded us what's important. It's not about who is right, it's not about getting to the right answer or agreeing. It is about listening—simply being calmer, clearer, and caring. You helped us accomplish this.

I learned by watching you grow up and from how you chose to work "hearter," not harder. You taught me a lot about how important it is to work from the heart. I'm still working on that lesson, thank you. When faced with questions or confronted with a challenge that I'm not sure about—is this the right decision for me, is this the right direction, am

I going to get stressed from this, is this going to produce results, is this going to create a conflict in my personal life, is this going to cause an imbalance, be insincere, or send me in an inauthentic direction—when I am not sure, I ask myself, "What would Ryan say or do?"

I love our chocolate field trips, Ryan, where we go to Louise's Belgian Chocolates and pick out your favourites. Or I come home on my own special field trip, and I pick up a little chocolate mouse for you. Or I hear you've gone to pick up chocolate for your girlfriend, and Louise informs me you dropped by and compliments me on what an amazing son I have. This is when I know that I'm doing a good job: When I hear from others what an amazing kid you are. I know parents can be biased, but you truly are a gift on this planet. You are a gift to the friends you have. We are proud of the way you choose your circle of friends. You are a gift to your girlfriend and to your future wife, whoever that may be, because you know how to cook, you know how to treat them well, you know how to deliver unconditional love. You are an amazing individual who is a gift to everybody you come in contact with.

Thank you, Ryan, for being in my life. I refer to you as an angel on earth.

You are a gift to me, and I look forward to every single day and every blessing you bring me.

I love you, Ryan, from the bottom of my heart.

Love,

Nonny

Pauline Fleming is the chief inspiration officer at Proactive Business Leadership as well as the mother of two. She is an active and loving mom as well as spouse to a Fortune 100 executive. She is one of only three people in the world to hold Certified Speaking Professional and Master Certified Coach designations. She is an outstanding author, coach, and professional speaker—visit her at www.leaderswhocare.com.

Your Decision ... My Life ...

My dearest children,

s the mother of five amazingly wonderful children, three of
whom have entered in "teenagerdom," I have spent countless
hours pondering their lives. It seems like just yesterday, they
were babies I could hold and protect. My decisions were as simple as
choosing a brand of diaper or what cute outfits they should wear that
day. I spent countless hours snuggling them, singing to them, bathing
them, feeding them, and just loving them....My dreams back then
consisted of who they would become and the kind of mother I wanted
to be. I dreamed of dance classes, sports teams, music lessons, and family
trips. I envisioned first days of school, taking the training wheels off,
and countless trophies on my mantel. Somewhere between rocking my
children to sleep and holding their hands to cross the street, they began
to grow into the wonderful people they are now. Time has slipped away
from me and I now realize they are beginning to make their own ways
in the world. Yes, I know that as young teenagers, they still need us. I
know that it will be a while before they are actually out of the house,
but really fourteen years have slipped by in the blink of an eye...the
next four years are not going to go by any slower.

In the everyday hustle and bustle of our crazy household, it can
be days before I get a decent conversation with them. They are busy
with their sports teams, school, youth groups, friends, girlfriends,
boyfriends, etc. I am a constant in their lives, which translates to
boring, not all that exciting. It doesn't occur to them to tell me

all the little things. I know that this is normal. In my heart, I am proud they are independent and are outgoing enough to create such fulfilling lives for themselves. In my soul, I know they are going to be fine in the long run; they are becoming strong and kind people. I also know that at this stage of my children's lives, they are supposed to be distancing themselves from me. This is the time in their lives when they begin to separate themselves from our family unit in preparation for adulthood. They will make new relationships, and at this time their dreams will start to take over where mine have left off. …

With all of this in mind, I want to make one point that I have said hundreds of times. I have told my children this in countless lectures and times of discipline. I have told them this in times of heartache and just as a spur of the moment sentiment: No matter how old you are, no matter where you go, even when you are grown up, married, and have children of your own, your lives will forever be linked to mine. Your lives are pieces of my own heart, given to you by me, your mother—the first person to ever love you, the first person to ever hold you, and one of the few people who will ever love you more than herself. Your lives will forever be directly reflected in my own. As you grow up, please remember this.

The time is coming when you will stop needing my permission for decisions you make. You will no longer need to be home by curfew. You won't have to tell me where you are going or who you are going to be with. I won't be able to tell you not to get into a vehicle with someone or not to place yourselves in danger. I won't be able to protect you and stop you from taking unnecessary risks. But as you grow, remember this: if you get harmed or if something happens to you, my life will be changed because of that. Because you are pieces of my heart, the decisions you make effect MY life too! So before you drink too much, or decide to try drugs, or get into a car that you shouldn't, before you text while driving, and before you make a bad decision, remember me, your mother. I loved you before anyone else. I don't want to lose you and the loss would strike a wound that could never heal. Your decisions...MY life. Your decisions...OUR lives.

Love,

Mom

My name is Kelly Burnett, and I am a married mother of five. I work full-time as an ER nurse as well, which has much to do with this letter. My job gives me constant reminders about how fragile life is. My children and husband are my life. They give me hope for a better world.

The Cord of a Legacy: Choose What You Will Bring

To my four amazing children, Danny, Jacob, Taylor, and Bailey,

I grew up without ever really knowing the love of a mother or father. I was raised by a struggling, single teenaged mother who was trying to find love herself. It's hard to be intentional about leaving a positive legacy to our children when you are in survival mode, but you leave a legacy regardless.

Good, bad, and ugly, we pass on to our children an emotional, relational, and spiritual legacy. It can be a beautifully braided cord of the three that ties us to our history and pulls us toward a wonderful future or a tattered rope that we can barely hold onto. The interesting thing about life and what God allows us to do is we get to choose what to take with us on our own journeys. I was thrilled to learn this early in my adult life. I chose to lay down the legacy of hurt, the legacy of discouragement, and the feelings of "not good enough." I also picked up a spiritual cord that I had never known.

I have worked hard to repair my own legacy and weave it into a cord of love to pass on to each of you. I want you to know that I love you deeply and would give my life for each one of you. I want you to know that when you face tough times, scary times, and times when you just can't seem to find your way out of life's fog, I am here to be a lighthouse and offer guidance and love.

I hope I have nurtured in each of you the seed of encouragement that gives you the confidence to reach for big dreams and bold adventures.

Don't settle for mediocrity. Run from it. Fight it with every fibre of your being. Climb a little higher than you thought you could and don't let dreams go unexplored. There is so much more of life to live than most people ever realize. I'm cheering for you.

Lastly, I hope you know that there is a God who loves you and that when you get that spiritual "cord" in order, the rest seems to be so much easier. You were meant for a relationship with Him, and until that is right you will continue to fill that void with other unhealthy things.

Now the choice is yours. You must decide what you will take on your journeys. What needs repair, what needs to be left behind, and what will you preserve and take along this life's road? Be intentional, because you will pass a legacy on to your children...good, bad, or ugly.

I love you,

Mom

Gina Schreck, CSP, is president at SocialKNX and an expert in social media marketing for businesses from hotel and retail to small businesses and franchisors. She is a loving and supportive mom who makes time for her four amazing children. Find out more about Gina at www.socialknx.com.

My Incredible Children

To my incredible children,

Yes, I love you all equally, but not the same…because you are not all the same. You are each unique and beautiful in a way that makes you, you. But I love you all equally. I know that I spend time with some of you more than others. I try to be with the one who really needs me at that moment in time; I don't always know that you need me, unless you tell me. You can tell me anything. Yes, I might get mad, be hurt, not understand…but I will always love you! After all, you inherited stupid things from me, so who am I to judge?

I know that it makes you crazy when I call just to check up on you, but I love you and I love the little people that you've brought into this world. For so long as I live I will call to check up on you or them when I feel a need to hear your voice. Yes, I can hear it in your voice when things are not going great for you. Remember sometimes things don't go great for me either…and sometimes I might not have the strength to carry you. But that does not mean I don't love you. It means I might need you.

Life has not been easy for our family. I wish that I could have given you all so much more. But I see now that the one gift your parents gave you was the strength to survive! Love! Love! And more love. Those are gifts that I pray you give your own children. The strength of a family is like nothing else on earth, and even though you may not always like your family, we love you!

On the day that your brother died…the universe tested the true strength and love of our family. Tommy is with us all, all of the time. He left behind a family better for loving him and for his love for us.

I could not have made it through those days without all of you. You carried me through, dragged me back to life, cried with me, gave me strength when I had none. But most of all, you, my children, gave me a reason to go on living. I am not sure I could have done that without the strength you shared. I will forever stand in awe of the people you've become.

Remember one thing...even the strongest people you know fall down, break down, slow down, let you down. Nobody can carry the weight of the world on their own shoulders. Everyone needs a helping hand some time or other. Even you! Never be afraid to share the weight you carry with your family...they will surprise you.

Cry in the rain. Nobody can see your tears there. It is the perfect time and place to clear your mind, mend your heart, heal your soul.

Never surrender your soul to anyone. Your soul is your very being and you, my children, are amazing souls.

For all the things I didn't do, for all the times I failed you or disappointed you, broke your heart or made you cry, or seemed so far away in mind or miles...know that I always, always loved you. Today, tomorrow, forever...I will always love you.

And yes, even after I've left this world, I will be there with you... dancing, playing, crying in the rain.

Mom xoxo

Rachel Curry is a mom and fantastic artist from the Studio in the Woods in Edmonton, Alberta. She loves to spend time with the loves of her life—her children and Tom, her loving husband.

The Strength of Seven Generations

My dear children,

You know, from the many times I've told you, that I spent much of my childhood on my grandparents' farm, learning to pick cotton, pull watermelons and cantaloupes, help my grandmother can tomatoes and beans, skin a catfish without getting stuck by its sharp fins, milk a cow, doctor sick animals, and hoe a row of corn. Everything was done by hand, even the laundry. It was a time of hard work, some scarcity, and of fixing things that broke.

Nowadays, not even small farmers still do things by hand. Cotton is picked and cows are milked by machine, combines plow and stack peanuts, and farms have electricity and running water with washing machines that any city dweller would be proud to have. Some things I learned on the farm I have passed on to you, and I see you do them, automatically, with your own children, which thrills me. I tell you now things to pay special attention to, passing down through our family's generations what I experienced in that heart-filling time: the simplicity and natural harmony of that way of life I hope we have in our family forever.

On the farm, I got to be out in nature—a lot. I went fishing in the creeks and ponds, lay in the pasture surrounded by cows, and watched the big cumulus clouds float by, drowning in a sea of blue sky and bathed in sun. Wherever I went, the farm dog went. My toys were piles of pine straw, cicada skins left on the pine trees in the moult, grasshoppers and lizards, and the current crop of kittens or puppies. When I gathered the eggs in the henhouse, I spent time enjoying the baby chicks. I learned about birth and death, as piglets and calves and puppies came into the world, and animals that were sick or severely injured were put out of their misery. I watched my grandmother set quail traps so she could make us a tasty wild dinner. I picked buckets and buckets of wild-growing blackberries so she could make them into a deep-dish pie, which after I ate it, left my tongue purple. Seasons, weather, cycles of life, animal behaviour, and growing nuts, fruits, and vegetables were all an integral part of my childhood.

Please pass this on to your children, and theirs after them—to seven generations! I did this with you by growing our organic garden every year, harvesting our twenty-two fruit trees and taking you backpacking in the wilderness at every opportunity. I know I drove you crazy at dinner, as I pointed out all that we were eating that we had actually grown in our own yard, yet I see the results of this as you now care for your chickens, turkeys, dogs, rabbits, and birds, while raising your own vegetable garden with my precious grandchildren. You, and they, are fearless around animals and have compassion and love for them.

On the farm, children went almost everywhere adults went. There was little differentiation between "work" and "life." It was all integrated, a whole. As a farmer, part of my grandfather's day would be to go into the garden and harvest tomatoes or butter beans or Crowder peas, to bring home to my grandmother so she could cook them for dinner or can them in jars for later in the year. Whether it was to find a lost cow, make sure the pigs had water, doctor animals infected with parasites, cure the tobacco in the barn, pull a stump out of the field, or fix the tractor, children were as much a part of what was going on as the adults. We helped the adults by running and fetching in support of what they were doing. Simultaneously, we learned how to work with others, take responsibility, and feel important, and how to care for and fix critters and machines. We were a community. Every person in the community was important; and the community was vital for everyone to support.

Involve your children in your lives, allowing them to be with you as much as you can. Teach them about what you are doing, allow them to help, and give them responsibility, even for the hard parts. It's what kids need to feel solid self-esteem, connection, intimacy, and good in their lives as part of our human community.

Children on the farm also had time to be alone. They could play together or spend time alone. But they didn't have an adult peering over their shoulder, scheduling "playdates" or making commitments for their child to be on a team or take a class. Our fun came from making up our own games, digging in the dirt, standing in the water as it poured off the eaves of the house in a downpour, playing with animals, or reading a good book under the pecan tree. So few children are trusted to be alone these days, yet that alone time is vital for looking inward, for sorting through what happens in life, and for finding out where one stands on an issue or experience, so DO safeguard your children's alone time!

And there were special times. Playing croquet on the lawn with the whole family, climbing in the magnolia tree (where we could see out, but adults had a hard time finding us), and Friday night fish fries that brought everyone together—even the neighbours. When I was five, the Easter Bunny visited the pine straw nest my grandmother and I created, leaving the most brilliantly coloured eggs! Celebrating New Year's, my grandfather and uncle set off fireworks in the pasture next to the house. It was so great to see them playing together. And sitting together on the front porch as we all shelled peas for canning or freezing gave us opportunity to talk together about the latest news, family events, future planning, and memories from long ago. Taking time to just be together as human beings is something that seems to be increasingly difficult in these days of personal technology, texting, and constant music. Remember to give your children the experience of family time and doing projects together, so they, too, can develop their basic humanity.

So much of who you are, and who you can teach your children to be, got started long ago on the farm, where children were an integral part of things, everyone played and worked together, and we cooperated with nature and living things. Keep these things close to you, to your children, and to their children as well.

As an adult, I returned to the farm for a visit. At dawn, I went to the pond with bait and fishing pole, paddling the rowboat to the middle. As the sun started to rise, I put down my pole and marvelled at the beauty, tears streaming down my face. I said aloud the words of my heart: "I found my soul on this farm, and I am so grateful!"

I pass that soul experience on to you, to your children, and to their children to the seventh generation. I am grateful to you for your part in this progression. I love you deeply.

Mom

Ilene Dillon had a challenging childhood that included the early loss of her birth mother and the absence of her father, constant moving with her military family, and various types of abuse. The one constant, stabilizing influence was the farm of her stepgrandparents, which she writes about here. Ilene is a California therapist, coach, parenting educator, professional speaker, author, and radio host. She has lived as a single, married, step-, and adoptive mother and is now grandmother of five. Ilene is married to neurosurgeon Dr. Robert Fink and lives in northern California. Visit her at www.emotionalpro.com.

Unexplainable Joy

Dear Nathalie and Jenna,

"If you live to be a hundred, I want to live to be a hundred minus one day so I never have to live without you."
—A. A. Milne, *Winnie-the-Pooh*

The moment you took your first breaths in this world, all of my dreams and aspirations for your lives to blossom emerged. That first look into your wondrous, innocent eyes filled me with a surge of love, a need to protect, and...unexplainable joy. You were perfect inside and out, and I promised that I would guide you to preserve this inner beauty, this inner light, and if you drifted away I would do everything in my power to help you reconnect.

I believe it's part of our life journey to stay connected or reconnect to that eternal "well" within. Life happens, and as children we begin to create beliefs about ourselves, other people, and the world. How, you may ask, do we create these beliefs? By experiencing incidents, watching others, and sometimes misinterpreting events as children.

Let me share with you the story of Me and the Bee. When I was four years old, my sister and I were playing in the backyard. I needed something in the house so I ran through the garage and tried to go inside. The door was locked. That was odd. Then I heard that horrific noise, *bzzzzzz*, and saw this monstrous bee heading right for me! I knocked harder and harder, screaming my little head off...and still no one opened the door. I was petrified. I then began to make up stories in my head of why my mother wasn't opening the door: "She mustn't love me...what did I do wrong?...Oh, I must be bad. There is this killer bee ready to torture me and she's not opening the door!" I don't even remember what happened except I didn't get stung by the bee. However, this memory was filed in my brain, with the story that I was unlovable.

My kid brain didn't have the ability to say to myself, "Self, maybe my brother is napping and I've already run in and out five times; or maybe she's just washed the floor and she doesn't want muddy footprints; or she doesn't know this monstrous bee is ready to attack me."

As children we don't have the logic or reasoning powers to see other possible perspectives. Developmentally we are as egocentric as young children and we perceive things relative to ourselves. The reality was that my baby brother was trying to sleep and my mom didn't want us running in and out of the house. Every single one of us creates these distorted stories and we start believing them. Year after year, we build on these stories until we have thousands of files stored in our memory banks. How silly is that? Unfortunately, these beliefs take us further and further away from that inner beauty.

My darling daughters, I know there are probably memories that you, too, have stored in your memory banks that contribute to your negative moods or behaviours. I wish I could take my magic eraser and rub them totally away. Awareness of these distorted stories is the cornerstone to returning to that inner beauty. Knowing every human being has them is the first step; next, please decide to shift them to reality and chalk it up to being human.

Some other words of wisdom I'd like to share are that you do not cause others unhappiness or happiness; anger or frustration; excitement or joy. Every single individual is their own "emotion control board." It's totally up to our selves how we feel and react to situations and people. I get that this is a difficult concept to grasp, understandably. Nonetheless, it's true.

The important thing to remember is that all emotions are acceptable, but not all behaviours are. When we don't accept our own emotions, we act them out with our children, friends, and family members in unhealthy ways. When our feelings control us rather than us being able to control them, we have a much harder time creating healthy relationships. If we perform inappropriate behaviours we do affect others; however, we are not responsible for their emotional reactions. This is the difference between influencing and controlling. We can influence others' emotions, but they're the only ones who control their emotions. And the reverse holds for us as well.

I will always remember one Mother's Day when you two made me breakfast in bed. I was a single parent at the time and you were eight and six years old. I could hear your giggling and whispering in the kitchen, trying to secretly create your gourmet breakfast. You bounded into my bedroom yelling *"surprise"* with peanut butter all over your hands and faces. I was so touched my eyes filled with tears of joy. Actually I did cry when I read your note: "Dear mommy, we made this brecfist by are sefe. Lov Nathalie + Jenna" (with the J reversed).

Obviously, I could have responded to the mess and noticed all the spelling errors in the note, thinking I was helping you advance in spelling. But I didn't. I could have screeched, "Get your sticky hands off my bed," but I didn't. Instead I pointed out the delicious toast, the beautiful flower, and all the hard work you put into everything. Your faces beamed with pride and my heart burst with happiness. It was my choice to feel this way, not yours. I was responsible for my feelings. Please grasp this concept as it will free you from many worries and hardships in your lives.

The great news is no one can make you feel anything.

The really fantastic news is you cannot make anyone else feel bad.

And the really, REALLY marvellous news is you can make yourself happy by adjusting the beliefs you learned through the eyes of a child that caused your misery.

Remember Gandhi's words of wisdom, "No one can hurt me without my permission."

I love you more than words can describe and I'll love you forever. Hold onto that inner beauty, believe in yourselves, and you will do your work on this planet with love, ease, and playfulness.

Love,

Mom

Cathy Lumsden, MA, is a dedicated mom, psychotherapist, author of The Best Advice Your Mother Never Gave You, *and TV host of* The Best Advice. *Her biggest joys in life are her two awesome daughters. www.thebestadviceyourmothernevergaveyou.com*

Life's Challenges Can Make You Better, Not Bitter

Dear children,

*I*f I can pass along one lesson, it is to ride the storms of life by confronting each challenge along the way with the attitude, "I choose to become better from life's challenges, not bitter."

Our family has had much experience along these lines, with the loss of your father at age thirty-eight in a car accident, the diagnosis of multiple sclerosis in my daughter and eldest son, and the tragic car accident that also caused my eldest son's paraplegia. My younger son also has an autistic son who needs much special care.

My dear children: Focus not on what you are powerless to change or control, but what you can do about it. And there is much to be done by you. The most important is to remind yourself that all families have challenges, and mostly you won't want to trade challenges with them! Be grateful and find the right and uplifting force inside to not only face these challenges, but also to overcome them by giving back to help others. There are always families less fortunate facing even more difficult times.

Love,

Mom

Jody DeVere is the CEO of AskPatty.com, mother of three, and grandmother of six. Jody runs a marketing to women agency providing automotive education to women consumers, as well as training, ongoing marketing support and education, and certifications to car dealers, independent service locations, tire dealers, collision centres, and other automotive retailers. As a social media marketing to women expert, journalist, car care expert, and safety spokesperson, Jody's primary goal has been to promote, mentor, and support careers for women in the automotive industry. She has more than twenty-five years of achievement as a successful entrepreneur focused on sales and marketing leadership to assist her in this quest.

My Whole World—My Girls

To my daughters, Haley, Gracie, Emily, and Natalie,

Haley, my first-born, you will always be the oldest. I was young and scared when you were born. I was worried that I wasn't going to be able to be a good mom. But you were such a good baby, you made it easy. I loved watching you grow and learn. You were so smart. You showed me that I was doing a good job. You love school, especially math. You make me proud. I love to watch you sing and dance, so full of energy. You are a great big sister, always watching out for your little sisters. Thank you.

Gracie, when you were born we were ready because we had learned so much from your sister. You were so cute with your blond hair and blue eyes, just like me. You are a sweet girl, you love animals and babies. You like to clean and tidy like me, too. You love school, especially reading. You are always trying to help me clean up. Thank you.

Emily, when you were born everyone said, "Another girl?" Yes, our third daughter. You were the smallest of the girls. So pink and cute. I just could not be disappointed; God gave us a healthy, beautiful baby girl. I felt blessed. You taught me about patience. You had numerous ear infections that first year. I didn't get much sleep, but sometimes when I was up rocking you in the middle of the night, I was grateful for the special time we had together. You are always happy and smiling. You are a cutie pie. Thank you.

Natalie, you are my baby girl. You completed our family. I am glad that you have three wonderful sisters to look up to and help lead you through life. I always wanted a sister. You are funny and cute. You love baking with me and eating the treats we make, too. You like to play with your sisters, but you like your alone time, too. You will always be my baby. Thank you.

I love my house full of singing, dancing, dresses, makeup, and hair bows. I wouldn't trade it for anything in the world. I love that you have taught me to be more patient, caring, loving, understanding, and responsible than I even knew I could be. You make me want to be a better person. I am grateful for all the special times we have had so far. I am excited for all the moments we will share as you grow from little girls into beautiful young women. I will be right here beside each of you every step of the way. I hope you all try your very best to be the best you can be. Work hard and make your dreams come true! You make me so proud. I love you more than words can say. I will always love my girls.

Mom

Chrystal Chisholm is a student at the NSCC taking office administration. She returned to school after eight wonderful years as a stay-at-home mom. She works to be a positive and inspiring force every day for her wonderful girls—and is doing it seamlessly.

A Mom to Boys, Just Feels Right

To my delightful boys,

Growing up in a family of all girls plus my dad, I had no expectation of what it would be like as the only woman in a home with all males. Nail polish and the brand of tampons are important to only me now. I will forever lose the battle over which channel to watch: TSN for me from now until eternity. I have no one to borrow hairspray or clothes from, and the toilet seat remaining up will be the new norm.

I had no idea when I had you boys just how much money I would spend on food, or how often and urgently you would require it. I couldn't have anticipated the smell from sweaty hockey gear and soccer cleats, or the constant barrage of kids at the door, or how many times you could remain interested in shooting a hockey puck at a net in the driveway, or how easily those pucks can dent a garage door.

Likewise, I had no idea how much I would love being a mom to boys, how I wouldn't miss pretty, pink dresses, Barbies, or teaching a daughter to apply makeup. Even after having my second boy, and realizing that girls weren't in my future, I said to myself, "A mom to boys, it just feels right."

I couldn't have known, growing up in a house with all girls, just how much love boys have for their moms. Sometimes I am overwhelmed with pride imagining the incredible young men you will surely become. And then I feel immense pressure, pressure to be the kind of woman in your lives that will encourage you to search for partners who are strong, but not so strong that you lose who you are. I want you all to find someone who brings out the best in you, and you in them.

But what I want you to know more than anything else is how much joy you have brought to my life. Joy in the routine of making you a huge stack of pancakes and returning an empty plate. Joy when you point to me after a goal, acknowledging my commitment to the sport you love. Joy in the hugs around my neck and even when you push me away for hugging a moment too long. You have brought joy to every day, to every moment, to every part of my life. And I can only say "thank you" for being great sons and including me in your "posse." I will try to remember to put the toilet seat up.

Love,

Mom

Tina Hennigar is a mom of two active and talented young men. Tina continues to serve customers through the sales department at family-owned and operated Lighthouse Publishing. She is dedicated to her community's success through events and projects. Check out her award-winning newspaper at www.southshorenow.ca.

The Teenage Years

To My Boys,

*a*s I write this, we have just had another teenage battle of wills over something that I am sure was important, but now can't remember what it entailed. It is during frustrations like these that I go to my cherished albums from your baby days and remember that there have been many battles before and there will be more to come, and that's okay. I also remember that I will forget the issues, but I will never forget the love that I feel for you when I look into your eyes.

I always knew in my heart that God would bless me with two sons. It was a long road on our way to becoming your parents, and on the day that each of you were born, I thanked Him for blessing me. And I continually thank Him for allowing me to be your mom.

You have brought me my greatest joys and my biggest heartaches. I have cried buckets of tears as I have driven you to the hospital for broken bones and stitches, while you have cried on my shoulder over broken hearts and over the regrets of harsh words and arguments. I have cheered you from the sidelines as you crossed the finish line, as you won the final match, made your big save, or scored the winning goal. I have rubbed your back when you were not feeling well, and I watched your eyes close as the dreamy night settled upon you.

I am truly amazed as I watch you develop, grow, and find your true selves. I am learning that the role of being a mother is so much more than what I originally thought. It is about discovering what lessons to teach and what details to ignore at any given stage, and that this can be where the greatest battles, heartaches, and joys can come from.

So as you transition from boys to men, I send you these lessons to ponder. Many of these form the strategies that I teach to my audiences because I believe in them so strongly, and I hope that they guide you as you choose your very own paths.

Be your own compass. You have the ability and strength to do great things if you choose to. You already have achieved so much, so don't let others determine if your goals are worthy of pursuing. Only you know if you are willing to put in the time, energy, and faith to achieve what you believe to be your true destiny and purpose.

Don't settle for less than leading a purposeful life. But know that to get to where you are going, and to ride the winds of destiny, you are going to have to muck a few stalls along the way. In other words, you can get to the top, but you are not going to start at the top.

Speak honestly and with compassion. Words hurt, and in our anger the words that we use may leave a crumpled heart in return. Don't assume that others know you appreciate and love them. You can never say those things too often.

Choose your partners well and know they give you a gift when they give you their hearts. Until you can cherish the feelings of others, know that you are not ready to be in a relationship.

Surround yourself with people you can truly count on. We all need family and friends to support us. Hang on to those who cheer you on and walk away from those who tear you down.

Get good at problem solving. It is far too easy to get stuck in being angry, jealous, frustrated, hopeless, or helpless. Move yourself forward by trying to figure out what you can and can't do to deal with whatever issue is in front of you.

Ask for help. You don't have to have all of the answers and others may have already invented that wheel.

Remember that very few things in life are black and white. There are so many shades of gray. Be open to other people's ideas and opinions, as their experiences of the world may be very different than your own and may contain possibilities you may not have thought of.

Though you may groan at the lessons I put forth, know that they come to you with love and with hope for your futures. I can see glimpses of the men you are becoming, and I am very proud. You are showing yourselves to be strong, self-assured, and passionate. You are brave and able to step outside of yourselves and try something new. And you are not easily influenced by the opinions of others, even when it means being ostracized by those around you. I really am so very proud.

I wish you lives full of passion, purpose, and possibility.

Love always and forever,

Mom

Beverly Beuermann-King is mom to Tayler and Nick and wife to Rodger. In her spare time, she is a stress and wellness specialist who helps individuals and companies that want to minimize the impact of stress, better control their reactions, and live healthier lives. www.WorkSmartLiveSmart.com.

Let's Walk in the Waves

my caiya,

*e*ver since i first imagined, then suspected, your little tadpole existence, i have loved you...i can still, twenty-four years later, close my
eyes and feel you dancing under my heart, and smell your sweet
baby self...when your newborn liquid eyes bore into my soul for the
first time, i felt the ferocious, primal knowledge that my heart was now
outside my body and with you, and it was both thrilling and terrifying ...

believing the old adage "it takes a village," i set out to surround you
with as many strong women as i could muster...with the eccentric cast
of characters who held you, in their arms and in their hearts, you always
had someone to go to, since i well knew my limitations—that i could
not be all that you might need or want...in this, we have served you
well, i think...

when you were four years old and entered preschool, you began to
question the concept of what it meant to be a family...your friends,
most having long ties to the small town in which we lived, spoke of
their cousins, aunts, uncles, and grandparents...you asked me what
"related" meant, and i explained...your eyes brightened, grew wide
in the classic "aha!" expression..."i get it!" you shouted, "nanny is our
family because she HAS to be...kate and jen are our family because we
CHOOSE-ED them to be...they are our choose-ed family!"...yes, caiya,
they are...

yours is an old soul...you told me stories, from the time you could
talk, of the lives you had lived before...i wrote them down, and have
them still...i think that is partly why you became such a talented and

passionate actor, able to slip into other personae and wear them like an old and well-loved shirt, and how you have been the author of such mature, poignant, and bitingly funny works of fiction—most written from the perspectives of much older voices ...

we felt our way through your childhood, stumbling occasionally yet always holding hands...we had rules—although if it was not an issue of safety, it was up for negotiation: play, create, ask questions, read, dance, be silly, practice random acts of kindness, let your curiosity lead you places, don't ever walk past our dogs without patting them...when you were eight months old we visited your grandparents...i asked my stepmother, your nana gwen, what she thought was the most important lesson to teach children...she thought manners, and while i believe they can cover a multitude of shortcomings, i think magic—how to look for it, find it, create it...i still believe this...and honesty; tell the truth—to others, and to yourself...make conscious choices, and own them... know that you may have to defend them...(a resounding question heard throughout your adolescence was, "was it worth it?")...spend time alone—not BY yourself but WITH yourself; discover your rhythms without the influences of, and reactions to, others...get to the truth of who you are..."no" is a complete sentence...volunteer—consider it rent for living on the planet and having the life you are fortunate to have... (you were allowed to choose where—but not if—you volunteered... this worked well for years, but eventually, at twelve, you realized that not everyone did this and you balked)...question everything, and look behind the facade...when you were five, we were extras in the movie *Simon Birch* being filmed in our town...we would arrive on set one day to a winter scene, with fake snow and barren trees, and the next day to a fall scene, with green grass and brightly coloured leaves magically back on the trees...the next day would be different again, and so on... it was an excellent lesson in critical thinking and reality versus fantasy, especially as portrayed in the media...you learned to look beyond, and to question ...

every year for your birthday you received a privilege—a ceremony of sorts, to celebrate your growing readiness for new experiences...you would bring me a proposal in the days leading up to your big day, and the negotiations would begin...you developed a deep self-awareness and mighty negotiating skills...(those came back to bite me later on ...)...i always had plan b ready in case i had to say no—which i didn't, until you turned fifteen...no caiya, you may NOT stay alone for the weekend... many of the problems we faced in those tumultuous teenaged days could be summarized by this: you were not as old as you thought you were and not as young as i thought you were ...

these are the things i know for sure, caiya: when in doubt—when you feel overwhelmed—just breathe...and do the next right thing...and then the next...hugs help, as does puddle-jumping, blowing bubbles, dancing, singing loudly with enthusiasm (doesn't matter if you don't know all the words), dodging waves, candles, a good book, and celebrations—always... an un-birthday, day of silliness—just celebrate ...

Elizabeth Berg wrote, and i love this, that "Along the way there will be rips and tears in the fabric of who you are. You will always notice the scar, but there is an art to mending. If you are careful, the repair can actually add to the beauty of the thing because it is testimony to its worth."

i love this journey, caiya, and i love you...come hold my hand and walk with me in the waves ...

mom

Trina Ladd, having lived on Canada's east coast all her life, has recently moved to British Columbia, where she is working at a homeless shelter and does outreach as well. Trina and her daughter, Caiya, continue to have many fine adventures and find magic everywhere they go.

Two Best Lights in My Life

Dear Todd and Tyler,

*O*nce upon a time many years ago a young lady was being blessed with the knowledge of having her first son, Todd. It was a time of joy, a time of fear of the unknown. To her amazement, besides taking her breath away, making her forget the pain, this blue-eyed wiggle settled into a warm cuddle in her arms.

A short time after her first blessing, she found herself giving life to another son, Tyler, who made her heart overjoyed with so much love, and he, too, formed that warm cuddle in her arms. Today, that is only a fond memory.

She then had two sons who grew over the years to amaze her with their abilities to be artistic and full of wit, adventure, and charm. There were times she was given away to their fearlessness, their strong minds. But always they were there to please her with their helpfulness, their open hearts to listen, and their understanding of their mother's many lonely life moments.

In my years of being a mom, truly some of the best years of my life, I may have overlooked some of your emotional needs, desires. I cannot make up for that now, but I can tell you both, from my heart, you are loved each day of my life. I held you when you were sick, and I gave what I had to give without hesitation. You grew not only to be brothers but also best friends. You followed each other through your growing years, experienced good music, hard play, and lasting friendships with others, your own individual thoughts. But you were always there for each other. Even today.

I sit and laugh today with the memories they have given me. One teaching the other to dance before the BIG date. The parties they shared while their dad and I were on holidays, only to find out the dog had eaten a hole in the sofa trying to retrieve a ball while the masses partied around him. The surprise birthday they gave their nana, who had never experienced one in sixty years. The wonderful cooks they have become, while I worked in a flower shop. They have carried on their culinary delights to their own families today. These are only some of my many memories that fill my "bottle."

Today, they are grown men. They have faced some of life's challenges, including the passing of their dad. Loss is never easy; it only makes you stronger. They have grown from it and now can be there for their own families in need.

Yes, they have found young ladies to share their different lives and build their own memories together. It hasn't been easy as distance has separated us all. They have given me four beautiful grandchildren: Tait, Emily, Nicholas, and Breton, that I cherish in my heart. I hope they, too, can fill their "bottles" with all the memories they will have over their lifetimes.

My "bottle" has overflowed over the years with happiness and tears of sadness. As a mom to you both, Todd and Tyler, I thank you for all the years of love you have given to make that "message in a bottle" so memorable.

Love you all forever,

Mom

And they live happily ever after.
The End

Sandy Sokolik is a retired florist and artist who was born outside of Montreal and studied for a short time under one of the Group of Seven. She has travelled the world with a backpack on her back—not in her twenties but rather starting in her fifties. She is an adventurer, an artist, and a mom who loves her boys very much.

May You Always Know …

To my beautiful daughters,

*M*ay you know above anything else how much you are loved.
I sometimes wonder…

What will you take with you from the years we spend together? When you go out into the world on your own, what will you carry? Who will you be? Will I have done enough?

Will the million kisses I will have placed on your tiny cheeks be enough to carry you through the hard times? Will the lessons I've tried to teach you be the right ones?

Will you know above anything else, how much I wanted you before you were here, how much my life changed in the second our eyes met, how truly cherished you are?

Will you know how much your mommy loves you? Will you remember what we say to each other before we go to sleep?

Will you have noticed as you grow the circle of love I've tried to build around you? The comfort I've tried to bestow on you and the peace I desire each of you to carry in your hearts?

I think you will. I think that above everything else, through the craziness of weekday mornings, the dance recitals, the camping trips, the car dances, the running through sprinklers, the game nights, the dinners, the arguments, the laughter, the tears, and the joy…I think you will know…I think you will hear my voice throughout your lives:

I love you precious Anneke. I love your smile, the way you make me laugh and the way you make me crazy. I love your jokes, your strength, and your fierce passion for life. I love your hugs and your bedtime saying.

I love the way you dance and sing, and that when you put your mind to something, you give it everything you've got! I love how loved you make me feel. And how lucky I feel to be your mom.

I love you sweet Molly. I love your pure heart, your cuddles, and your beautiful tears. I love your strength and your creative mind. I love your compassion for people and the way you let your heart lead you in life. I love your wisdom and your kindness. I love your humour and your quiet strength. I love the way you dance and play the ukulele and how underneath there's a girl who loves to be wild and is starting to really know herself. How blessed I am to be your mom.

I love you darling Sophie. You came into our lives and made us all feel complete. I love your giggles and your dimples. I love your connection to Mother Earth, to the water, to the Moon, and to animals and rocks. I love how you love everyone and make anyone at all feel at ease and happier than before they met you. I love that you call me mama and the hilarious sense of humour you have already at age three. I love how you make me feel. And I love how happy I am to be your mama.

May you always, always, always know how much you are loved my precious children.

Love,

Mom

Karen Nancarrow is a teacher who specializes in learning disabilities and loves helping mentor teachers and teach kids. She is in an amazing relationship and has the pleasure of being a mom to three wonderful girls. Being a mom is her favourite thing to do, the thing that makes her who she is, and the reason she gets up in the morning. Her children have taught her, loved her, and changed her.

A Gift from Halfway Around the World

Dearest Casey,

My journey to becoming your mother began long before you were born. While your father and I were dating, we talked about how we envisioned our future family. I had always felt very strongly and positively about adoption and once I had shared these feelings with your dad, we decided that adoption was going to be a part of our future.

Your big brother, Jaeger, made us parents a year and a half after we were married. When he turned one year old, we began the process to adopt our second child. Our personal experience with international adoption consisted mainly of families who had adopted daughters from China, so we decided we would also follow that route. Little did we know that fate had a very different plan for us!

In order to become an adoptive family, we were required to take part in an intense home study during which a social worker visited our home, asked us questions about our lives, and deemed whether or not we were fit to be parents. Once we received approval from the powers that be, our wait began. We waited and waited and waited for nearly two years, but no referral for a child came. The international adoption program in China was coming to its end, and the only thing we could be certain of was that it would be years before we received a referral for our child.

With heavy hearts and many tears, we decided to withdraw our application to adopt from China. At about the same time, we were invited to attend an informal meeting of families who were either in the process of adopting or had already adopted from Ethiopia. Within a matter of minutes, we realized that all of the time, energy, and tears spent thus far on our adoption journey had brought us to this very moment, to this very group of people, and to the decision to start the process all over again, but this time to bring a son home from Ethiopia. After a few adjustments to our original home study, our wait began anew.

Adoption is a true test of one's patience and sanity. Unlike a pregnancy, where at the end of nine months a baby arrives, there are no certainties, there is no timeline of expectations. Every single day when I woke up, I thought, "Today could be the day I see my son's face for the first time. Today could be the day I get THE CALL." Every day I wondered if today was the day my son was being born on the other side of the world. I wondered what you looked like, what you smelled like, if you were being cared for properly, if you were getting enough hugs and kisses.

Then one day in July, the phone rang. Our social worker's voice on the other end of the line said the words we had been waiting for so long to hear: "Your proposal has arrived. We have a baby for you!" I called your dad and we met at home to open our precious envelope and there you were, our tiny, beautiful, perfect two-month-old baby boy! I finally knew what you looked like. I finally knew your name.

And so, this part of our wait was over, but the most difficult, most emotionally exhausting, most frustrating wait was just beginning: the wait until we were able to travel to Ethiopia and hold you in our arms and bring you home to be with us forever. With the passing of every month, we received photos and a written update showing and telling us how much you had grown, how many teeth you had, what developmental milestones you had reached. It was almost more than I could bear, knowing that someone else was feeding you, bathing you, rocking you to sleep on a continent far away from me, your mother.

We waited for six long months, the longest months of my lifetime. I carried your photos with me everywhere I went and showed them to everyone I met. I would study babies around your age at the grocery store or the mall and imagine what it would feel like to hold you in my arms. I loved you so much and I hadn't even met you yet. Finally, a few days after Christmas, we received word that your travel visa had been approved and we were free to bring you home. We made arrangements to travel as soon as possible and within days we were on our way to Ethiopia and to you!

I will never forget the first moments we had with you on that very first day we met. Your caregiver appeared with you in her arms and handed you to me. You were real! You were beautiful! You were my son! You had the most amazing, inquisitive, searching, big brown eyes I had ever seen. I couldn't wait to get to know you and for you to know me. You adored your big brother, Jaeger, from that very first meeting and he was so thrilled to finally have his baby brother!

Our family has been complete since that day. I have had the great privilege to be made a mother by both biology and adoption and the love I have for each of my sons is equal, unconditional, and boundless. My sweet Casey, I may not have carried you in my womb for nine months, but I carried you in my heart for much, much longer. I could not imagine my life without you in it. I love you, my son.

Love,

Mommy

Teri Appleby lives with her husband, Keith, and their two sons, Jaeger and Casey. Her passions include travelling the world with her family, interior decorating, yoga, and running half-marathons.

A Collection of Thoughts

Kaitlyn, Kara, and Andrew,

I am so happy you are in my life. I want to hold you close, but I know I have to let you go. I want to give you everything, but I know that things are not the answer.

If I could give you anything, it would be everything you need to have a wonderful life. This letter is a collection of my thoughts and others' thoughts I have picked up along the way that have resonated with me. I hope, in some small way, this letter will mean something to you or help you when you need it. These are gifts money cannot buy and without which money means nothing, gifts that no one can give you and also gifts no one can take away.

If I could give you everything, I'd give you the gift of:

Time

To make the most out of life we must take time to live as well as make a living. The time we spend with those we love is the most important time of all. Take time to love and be loved. Take time for friendships and family, talks by the fire and walks under the stars.

Take time for laughter and hugs.

Take time for nature; enjoy the sunrise, the sunset, birds, the ocean.

Take time for solitude, time to be quiet and alone with your thoughts.

Take time today just for yourself. Today will never come again. Make the most of today and celebrate all that you are.

Take time for good books and great conversation.

Take time to give of yourself and your talents so that you can make a difference in the lives of others.

Take time to daydream, help a stranger, visit a friend, or just play.

Time is more valuable than money. You can always get more money, but you can't always get more time.

Wealth and Abundant Thinking

Dream big and follow your dreams. If you knew without a doubt that your dreams were coming true what would you do to get ready? (Do it.) How would you celebrate your accomplishments? (Do it.) What would you write in your gratitude journal? (Do it.) How would you pay it forward? (Do it.)

Wealth is the paucity of need; look it up. It's not what you make but what you get to keep that matters. It's not what you have but what you do with what you have that matters.

There is nothing you can't have or do or be. You are amazing! You are unlimited potential. Always aim higher than you believe you can reach—you will amaze yourself. Hold true to your dreams. Show the world how wonderful you are.

Along the Way

Create your own world. Do what you do well and with all your heart. Study hard, work smart, be honest, have integrity, be organized, talk gently, respect others, give the benefit of the doubt, look on the bright side, make the most of every day, believe in your dreams, look for opportunities to grow.

Don't settle for anything less than everything you want. Make it happen!

When you're struggling over a difficult decision take the "rocking chair test." Imagine you're ninety years old and looking back on your life—will you regret doing this or not doing this? Think about the impact of your decision in the next five weeks, the next five months, and the next five years. Make a decision based on your best information and have no regrets.

Use what you've got—talent, brains, health, gut feelings, wealth, friendships, time, joy, stuff. You are special. You are unique.

Take responsibility for your actions.

Take joy from random acts of kindness—do things for those who will never be able to repay you.

Before you go, I just want to make sure you to know how very much you are loved and what joy you have brought to my life.

Love you always and forever, more than the last number.

All my love,

Mom

Susan Sweeney is an author, speaker, consultant, and coach, but her most important roles are as a proud and loving mom to her amazing kids, Kaitlyn, Kara, and Andrew, and as a happy wife of their dad, Miles. Susan and Miles live in Waverley, Nova Scotia, and Fort Myers, Florida. Visit her at www.susansweeney.com.

Memories of My Son

*I*t was a beautiful spring day when you were born, my son. The day went on, a peaceful atmosphere was in the air, the skies were blue, and the flowers bloomed everywhere. It was a beautiful day. In the afternoon you decided it is time. After three hours you made your first sound in this world.

You took it easy even then, as you did all your life. Eventually the doctor had to pull you out, to help you push your way into this world. I remember the first time I saw you. I couldn't help it and laughed at how you looked. Your head was long like a cucumber. This was the result of the vacuum machine they used to help you get born. It disappeared after a few days and your head got to be the beautiful head you had, with its long blond hair and amazing face that made all envy you, the face that made girls melt at the sight of you. We named you Asaf. Asaf is our second son.

You had tons of charm, charm that let you go smoothly through life.

You were a typical teenager, and we had our share of fights. Well, maybe not typical. You were more stubborn than others and knew exactly what you wanted and how to get it. When reasoning didn't help, you put that amazing charm to work.

I remember one argument we had. You wanted to be mobile and decided a motorcycle would do the job. I was terrified and didn't agree. Being your mother, I knew to resist that charm that made others fall at your feet. I said "No, that's final." You stood there, looked me in the eyes and said, "You worry about a motorcycle. Well, I may board a bus and get killed from a terrorist bomb."

This made my stomach turn. Looking back, I am not sure if you just tried to make me angry and give up, or if you knew something with your sixth sense, something that we couldn't see, couldn't believe.

This sixth sense seems now like something that helped you enjoy life more, as though you knew your life would be shorter than we expected and that you needed to grab and enjoy every second of it. You took life very easy. School was a place to meet friends; meeting friends and going to parties was your main attraction. Surfing was a hobby that you spent lot of time at. You lived every minute as if it were your last.

Looking back, I can see now how you made the most of your short life. I just hope that you were happy and that we didn't manage to spoil that with our demands and restrictions.

I wish we had given you more, I wish we had let you do more things you wanted. I wish we could have made you happier then you were.

With each of your brothers, we had our share of problems: school, friends, moving, health issues. With you it seemed like nothing bothered you, like nothing mattered, like nothing had an effect. You were loved by all and admired by all. I remember how we came back after two years abroad. We all were exhausted, bothered, unpacking and working. You went out and after five minutes with your old friends, it seemed like you were never away. You were happy and in the centre of the group, telling all your friends about your experiences.

Out of all our travel experiences I will never forget our visit to Paris, to Versailles Palace; the place was packed with visitors, hundreds of people in line waiting to go in. The tour inside was slow, a huge line of people moving slowly from one room to the other, looking, photographing, reading the signs. There were dozens of rooms, if not more, in different colours, shapes, and styles. You were nine years old and got bored really fast. After a few rooms you moved ahead quickly, and soon I couldn't see you. I wasn't worried. I knew nothing bad would happen to you there, so we continued to move with the crowed.

After some time a buzz started, and we saw that somewhere ahead a crowd was building, all the tourists taking pictures at one room in particular. The line moved even slower than usual. It took us a while to get there, and when we got around the corner, you were there. You had crossed the line tourists were not supposed to cross and were lying on this fabulous Louis XIV sofa, your head and beautiful blond hair on one arm rest, your feet on the other, eyes closed, like nothing (and especially hundreds of tourists and their flashes) could disturb your peace.

We were embarrassed and took you out of the palace. We couldn't be mad with you, so we all laughed and had a nice time outside in the gardens and the park. I can't forget the image of you peacefully lying there, not impacted by the noise, crowd, or the importance of the place.

I am struggling every day, every moment to fill my memory with those happy thoughts of you alive, because I can't allow the memories of the last day to overtake me.

March 5, 2003, was a beautiful spring day. On that day an Islamic terrorist boarded a city bus in our hometown of Haifa, Israel. My son Asaf, almost seventeen years old, was on the bus coming back from school. The terrorist exploded the bomb that was strapped to him. Seventeen people died, nine of whom were schoolchildren. My dear and beautiful son Asaf was killed on spot. Asaf's dad was on a business trip out of the country that day and I was alone. I heard about the blast, but initially I wasn't worried. I couldn't think anything would happen to us; I couldn't believe that we would get hurt. It took a short time to get the first phone calls and news, till I got the one I dreaded. Asaf's girlfriend, who was with him on the bus and got off one bus stop before the blast, called to tell me he was on the bus and where exactly he sat.

I ran home, hoping somehow it was all a mistake and I would find Asaf watching TV with his phone turned off or sleeping on the couch. He wasn't home. The house was empty.

I then went to the hospital to try and find him wounded, in any condition, but just alive. All my hopes were denied. I was sent to the national morgue to get a final verification. At 2:00 A.M. I got the horrible news that Asaf was identified as one of the killed teenagers.

The next day the skies turned black and it started raining. In the afternoon we buried our beautiful son. I never got to see him.

I miss you so much my loved son.

Lea Zur is Asaf's mother. She is from Haifa, Israel. She is fifty-four years old, a software engineer, born in Israel, and the mother of four sons. Asaf, her second son, died in 2003 in a terrorist attack. Two years later, in 2005, she had another baby boy, Eithan, who fills her heart with joy.

Mom's Memories

Dear Lorilee, Marles, Jeremy, and Amee,

I remember gazing in awe while you slept in my arms and marvelling at the reality of being a mom. Each one of you captured my heart as your tiny fingers curled around mine and my journey into motherhood began anew. Now you are all grown up. My arms can no longer snuggle you close, but I still hold each of you tightly in my heart, surrounded by my love.

As I write you this letter, so many memories crowd into my mind. Some flit by while others require closer examination. I have shared many stories over the years, which add to the fabric of our family traditions. Some of your memories exist simply because you have listened to the countless retelling of events.

There are bittersweet memories that shaped my journey of motherhood, memories of almost losing each one of you before your first birthdays. Lorilee, my world almost shattered as I listened to you gasp for each breath while croup ravaged your lungs. Even the doctor did not know if you would live through the night. Tears flowed freely at thoughts of my empty arms. I had never felt so helpless. You miraculously recovered, and I held you close, hoping to never again face anything so scary.

Yet not even two years later, I watched you, Marles, as the reaction to your DPT shot spread a rash across your body and threatened to close off your airway. I wept and prayed for your survival, knowing the nearest hospital required a two-hour plane ride to reach, two hours you did not have. But you also survived with no lingering side effects.

After two close brushes with death I felt I could handle anything else life threw my way. But Jeremy, my son, I never knew if you would live long enough for me to meet you. Would you survive the accident's effects on my body while I still carried you under my heart? Seven months later I held you as you kicked and squirmed. I watched your adventuresome spirit as you grew to an adult with children of your own.

Amee, you scared all of us by not breathing for over seven minutes after your birth and then needing resuscitation more times than I can remember before lapsing into a coma. Nothing prepared me to stand in the neonatal unit watching your struggle to survive. Yet God allowed us to take you home sooner than the doctors expected. Our family life turned upside down while we helped you deal with the effects of the stroke, which extended into your adulthood.

Despite the depth of these tough memories, they only tell part of the story of your lives and mine as your mom. Memory-making moments both planned and spontaneous created many happy stories. Game time has been a source of laughter and mostly good-natured rivalry since you were all old enough to try simple games. Many times you older girls remained frustrated at attempts to play with your little brother and your cousin since the rules changed at their whim. Watching the two of them play by themselves proved hilarious. If they had only written down their variations on multiple games at once or new rules they invented, they might have made a fortune. Now the retelling brings laughter to present-day family game time.

I enjoy watching you implement traditions with your families. Traditions like the birthday person being celebrated as they choose their favourite meal and cake. I enjoy the continuation of the Christmas Eve tradition where every person in the house, regardless of age, puts out a stocking in hopes of pleasant surprises early the next morning. I revel in watching you be excited about simple pleasures and possibilities.

I willingly shivered in ice rinks as a hockey and ringette mom, breathed in the chlorine-filled air at the pool, listened to notes played not quite right on various instruments, and waited expectantly for the race results to be announced. I cheered, sometimes out loud but always internally, each of your accomplishments both inside and outside the classroom. Tears of joy flowed as I watched each of you in turn walk across the stage to receive your high school diploma. I truly believed you could be whatever you chose to be.

You older girls remember and laugh with me while recalling the adventure of camping with our friends. Two moms and eight children aged two to nine provided fun and laughter at the time and years later. Campfires, roasting marshmallows, and exploring new parks gave us leisure time to spend together as a family and formed good memories. Adventure waited with each trip, but occasionally those adventures caused us to play the "what if" game. I think some of you actually remember the camping trip interrupted one night by gunshots being fired close to the tent you slept in. We discovered how nine people could sleep in the camper, at least when seven of them were children and young teens. Survival, with no ill effects, allows us to look back and chuckle at the event.

Laughter and cheers coexist with tears and heartache in my memory banks of motherhood. Band-Aids and hugs dealt favourably with the inevitable cuts, bruises, and scrapes that accompanied childhood play and adventure. Some more serious injuries—like broken bones garnered while learning to play hockey, or a badly burned arm from spilling boiling water I had told you to stay away from—caused greater physical pain for you and anguish for my mother's heart.

Being your mom brought a dream to reality, but it did not come with a step-by-step instruction book. Each of your unique personalities and energy levels challenged me to learn methods to motivate or discipline you effectively. Some things succeeded while others failed miserably. What worked with one did not always work with all of you. I never dreamed a major attitude adjustment could happen by messing up a child's room, but desperation sometimes forced creative solutions. As you grew up, advancing from one stage of life to the next, I did not always adapt my mothering role quickly enough. Too often I lagged behind your need to assert more independence, and relationships suffered. I continue to learn that I do not have a big enough Band-Aid to help heal emotional hurts, missed friendships, or the hard choices you have all been forced to make at various times.

As I close this letter to you, my children, the most important thing I need you to know and remember involves love. No matter how old you become, no matter if I agree with your life choices and decisions, I have always and will continue to love each one of you more than my words can express. You are my twice given, treasured gifts from God.

All my love,

Mom

Carol Harrison is the mom to four adult children, the youngest of whom has special needs. She is a wife, a mother, and a grandmother to eleven children. At a very young age she came to know Jesus Christ as her personal Saviour. She has written and received critical acclaim for her writing and speaking. Check out her book Amee's Story *and her website at www.carolscorner.ca.*

Multiply It by Infinity

Dear Becket,

I am trying to find a way to tell you how much I love you.

There was a night recently when we were travelling, when I was awake all night in our London hotel worrying how I could describe it to you.

My love for you is deeper than the deepest depth, wider than forever, and cannot be described through art or music.

The only thing I can think that comes close is to tell you to watch for something: One day,

When you are riding on the bow of a boat on a crystal clear turquoise-blue lake, like Higgins Lake, in the late afternoon...

Watch for the sunshine on the water.

Watch for the brilliance, the magic of the sun as it slowly sinks closer and begins to waltz with the breathtaking beauty of the pristine lake.

Watch how the bright golden and amber flashes of light slam-dance off the tops of the azure waves and ricochet around the happy faces and bright smiles of the friends you are with.

Feel the coolish breeze in your impossibly messy/curly inherited hair.

Watch the sky and the water and the faces filled with laughter glistening like God has sewn golden sequins all around you.

When you feel the joy of that moment, multiply it by infinity…
That begins to come close to how much I love you.

Love,

Mama

Tami Evans is a full-time mama and according to her young son, Becket, she makes the best avocado sandwiches on the planet. Tami's career has ranged from stand-in for Melanie Griffith to university professor and fashion designer for Banana Republic to professional speaker. Find out about this amazing speaker, author, and mom at www.tamievans.com.

Kindness Counts

Dear Kathleen and Alex,

I'm writing this on your forty-fifth birthday, Kathleen. It seems incredible to me that my children are middle-aged women. Wasn't it just last month you were making furniture for your dollhouse?

When you were little, I thought it was my responsibility to teach you the unwritten rules of our society so that you would mesh comfortably with others, but also to help you grow into independent thinkers, so you would be able to manage life's inevitable challenges. Those aren't bad ambitions for a parent, but I think if I were to do it again, I'd say to myself, *I just want them to be kind.*

I think kindness was taught to me from such a young age I didn't realize how crucial a human trait it is. "Be ye kind one to another," I heard in Sunday school; "Help other people every day," I recited in Brownies; "Serve others," I vowed in CGIT. They say we believe what we hear over and over, but we also take it for granted. I certainly did. Being kind was "nice," and that was that.

Now I believe kindness is the essence of being happy, of being human. Anthropologists think we may be genetically programmed to be compassionate, so there's some scientific support for my belief, but I'm basing it on life experience. When serious illness and death blight your days, or when you make a dreadful mistake that can't be fixed, or when you fail at something that matters enormously to you, as inevitably happens to most of us, kindness will help you through the misery. There's a reason most of the world's great religions espouse kindness! Plato once quoted Socrates as saying, "Be kind, for everyone is fighting a hard battle."

When we are kind, we forgive others their mistakes, and through that, learn to forgive our own. That means we live in harmony with ourselves and with others. Imagine a life with no stress! I know, stress has been touted as a great motivator, but I think that accomplishing goals because you want to, instead of feeling driven to, is healthier—and a lot more fun! When we practice consistent kindness, we send negativity and anger packing. We never feel like victims, and we never victimize others. We feel good about ourselves and about our place in society—just as I wanted you to feel when I was "bringing you up." When we're kind, we live in a better world, inside and out, that we've helped create.

Genuine kindness is a source of delight, too. Your Nana, my mother, modelled this for us, didn't she? Her pleasure in others' accomplishments multiplied her own pleasure tenfold. And as a result of her attitude of joy in others, she had true friends of all ages to the end of her almost-ninety-nine years of life, even though most of her own family and peers had died. You both were her great friends as well as her beloved granddaughters, so you know what I'm saying is true. Comfort and joy flowed to and from her, because of her essential kindness.

Of course it's impossible to be perfectly kind—if it were, we'd likely never make the types of mistakes that require forgiveness! But we can practice "every day," as the Brownies promise, and be gentle with ourselves and with others—we all slip up.

You're both very kind women, so you are likely wondering why I'm writing about this to you. As your great-grandfather, your Nana's father, said to her when he was in his seventies: "You just figure out how to live life, and it's time to go!" I identify with him, so I'll just be kind with my slow self, and think I'm figuring it out now. And because it's taken me so many years to come to this deep appreciation of "the milk of human kindness," I thought I'd share.

Lots of love,

Mom

A retired actor and teacher, Janet Barkhouse has turned to writing. Her poems and short stories have been published in anthologies and literary journals across Canada. She has also published two children's books, and is working on a third.

Carrying Strength

Dear Maggie,

*A*s I sit to write this letter, I can feel you squirming in my belly. It is amazing to be nurturing your growth through me. With each day that passes, I get more and more excited to welcome you into this world and to get to know you. For many years you've been just a dream, but now that your due date is approaching, I want to share with you just a bit about your journey.

You are a wish that your father and I have shared for years. Since we became a couple, we've hoped to have children. Our desires were put on pause five years ago when I was diagnosed with breast cancer. When the diagnosis came, it was not the cancer that broke our hearts, but rather the disappointment that we may never be able to welcome our own children into this world. It was a heartache that most of our friends and family found hard to understand, so we had years of loneliness as we wrestled internally with the possibility that one of our biggest dreams in life may never be fulfilled.

It was with a mix of surprise and joy that we discovered that we were pregnant after consultation, support, and a little help from an incredibly dedicated medical team. We took the first few weeks in stride as we know that those can be difficult times for developing babies. At just about three months into our pregnancy, we received the distressing news that the doctors had again discovered a tumour in my breast that was likely cancerous. Our happiness had suddenly been replaced with fear and worry; we couldn't believe the unfortunate luck we'd been dealt.

Again, a team of amazing doctors stepped in and took the best care of you and I. By the time you had been growing for four months, a lumpectomy had determined that the mass was not cancerous. We were once again overjoyed, albeit still a bit reserved.

Just a couple of years before my original diagnosis, my mother (your grandmother) had also been diagnosed with breast cancer. She showed amazing strength throughout her struggle with the disease, and it was because of the courage that she had shown that I knew I could defeat the illness as well. We worry that the type of cancer your grandmother and I fought will be one that you will have to battle too. We already know, though, with what you've been through in this pregnancy, that you are a tough little girl, and we can only imagine that you will grow to be an amazing woman, full of strength.

Many years ago, as your father and I dreamt of the future, we decided that if we were ever lucky enough to have a little girl, we would give her the name "Maggie," short for Margaret, your grandmother's name. After the struggles of the past few years, we know that there is no better name for you to carry on in our family, and we hope that you will do so with pride.

You have now been thriving for thirty-five weeks, and before long we will be welcoming you into this world. We have watched you grow and develop through many ultrasounds and checkups and are getting anxious to meet you! I know that you will make your debut when you are ready, and when that moment comes I want you to know that I will welcome you into my arms with the love of a dream come true.

With much love,

Mom

Connie Bird is a mid-thirties mom-to-be and cancer survivor. She lives lakeside in rural Canada with her husband and dog. When not busy with teaching, she loves to spend time baking, crafting, or exploring the outdoors with family and friends.

Mom's Message in a Bottle

Danelle, Ionnie, and Malachi:

*C*onstructively speaking, I agree with Charlie T. Jones, author of *Life is Tremendous*, when he said, "You will be the same in five years as you are today, except for two things, the books you read and the people you meet."

The books you read

I will never forget. It was 9:00 P.M. on December 31, 1979: New Year's Eve. Your dad and our friends decided to go out to celebrate the New Year, and I decided to stay home and begin to read Napoleon Hill's book, *Think and Grow Rich*. But as I read, the book began to read *me*. I revealed, resurrected, re-energized, reassured the God-given potential in many areas of my life that I had never known or had forgotten were in me. The book helped me to understand how to set and achieve goals and dreams while living life on purpose. It all started with the method by which *desire* for riches can be transmuted into its financial equivalent, which consists of the following actions known as the Six Steps to Riches:

First. Fix in your mind the exact amount of money you desire. It is not sufficient merely to say, "I want plenty of money." Be definite as to the amount.

Second. Determine exactly what you intend to give in return for the money you desire. (Producing some kind of product or service to market.)

Third. Establish a definite date when you intend to possess the money you desire.

Fourth. Create a definite plan for carrying out your desire, and begin at once—whether you are ready or not—to put this plan into action.

Fifth. Write out a clear, concise statement of the amount of money you intend to acquire, name the time limit for its acquisition, state what you intend to give in return for it, and describe clearly the plan through which you intend to accumulate it.

Sixth. Read your written statement aloud, twice daily: once just before retiring at night and once after arising in the morning. As you read, see, feel, and believe yourself already in possession of the money.

This process is not limited to money but can be applied to every area of your life. Whatever you can see, feel, and believe in your heart, give it time, energy, and commitment to a plan of action while employing these steps, and you can achieve it.

As a result of this Mastermind Masterpiece, my inheritance to you is our McNeill Family Mastermind Group which we have formed, starting with our family mission statement, which reads as follows: "We are happy and we have fun together. As a family we are loving, peaceful, patient, and kind to each other. Our generosity is shared with others and we live a life of significance while leaving a family legacy."

Think and Grow Rich has helped us to create goals in ten different areas of our lives, including spirituality, family, finances, health, education, personal development, business/career, recreation, civics, and creativity. We set these goals for six months and one, five, ten, and twenty years into the future.

The people you meet

This book took me back to The Book (the Bible) and introduced me to many heroes, heroines, and people that I have met vicariously and in person along my life's journey. The Book has helped to give me a guidepost for living and for respecting and valuing others along the way as I learn how to try the spirit *by* the spirit. Equally as important, The Book reintroduced me to the greatest inheritance gift my mom,

Alberta Cobb, gave to me. Her gift was the introduction to the Giver of Life, her Lord and Saviour. She did not leave any material possessions, but the gift of life was what she shared.

So the inheritance and legacy we leave is the life we live, a life of service above self and in the service of others. This is demonstrated from the small investments of time into our family over a long period of time, which has already began to yield the fruit of the spirit of the inheritance you all speak to share: Danelle McNeill, as "My Queen of Toastmasters," Ionnie McNeill, as "The Baby Billionaire," and Malachi Munroe, my fourteen-year-old grandson, as "the li'l technology professor."

My inheritance to you all is the gift of sharing what you are reading and sharing your spiritual inheritance: the gift of giving of your time, talents, and treasures to worthy causes and to the people you meet.

Ann McNeill is a work-life expert, professional, coach, and author who works with entrepreneurial, professional, and executive women, helping them get greater clarity in their highest-income producing area of their businesses and lives. Ann, known as the MasterBuilder (building stronger and better lives), is the founder of MCO Construction, Constructively Speaking, International Mastermind Association, National Association of Black Women in Construction, and MCO Consulting. Connect with Ann at annmcneill.com.

Blake and Sean:

*I*ve been lucky to bear two sons. As a mother you want to protect, hold, cuddle, train, and, yes, even smother your children at times.

When you were babies, I held you and loved on you as often as I could. When you were toddlers, I watched you learn to crawl, then walk, and then run away—quickly. Often you'd bump into things and I'd want to smooth your landing. When you started school for the first time, I was both excited and sad to see you venture into the world without me holding your hand.

As I reflect on my own life, I realize that some of the most important moments, relationships, learning, and outcomes have been determined at the "intersections" of my life. These aren't traffic inter- sections or even points at which you must make huge, life-impacting decisions, but rather the small decisions that lead us down a path that ultimately contributes to our health, wealth, success, and happiness. I believe these are divinely inspired intersections and can be influenced both by you and by God.

Blake, as a teen you've tested the bonds between us, and when you were a young adult I often watched with trepidation as you drove away. Now, as you are entering college, you'll be boarding airplanes, carrying your own luggage, and making your way in the world.

Sean, you've been excitement and adventure even from birth, which was very risky. As you know, yours was a difficult pregnancy, and I was in the hospital for about nine weeks waiting and wondering if and when we would even see you. You've not given me a lot of rest since then either! True to form, you take risks, explore, and keep all of us active.

As you both grow older and more independent, it has been a joy to see you learn, grow, and do more. However, even though you're becoming independent, it's still sometimes a challenge to let go. As you venture out into the big, wide world I want you to know that I have been and always will be praying for you at the intersections.

The following is my advice for creating your own intersections.

First, be open to possibilities. Intersections present the possibility for learning something new, meeting a new person, or connecting to a group that could be beneficial to your personal or professional interests in the future. As an example, several of my best friendships and most successful business relationships have come from choosing to attend meetings. These intersections may not initially appear to be life-changing; however, attending can result in great friends and wonderful connections. Sitting by the "right" person can lead to marriage, life-long friends, mentors, and many other opportunities.

Second, be available. Be willing to step outside your comfort zone, make commitments and always keep learning. Walk through life with your eyes wide open, constantly looking for the connections and the intersections that abound. If you seek these intersections and opportunities, you, too, will find them.

Thirdly, choose to engage. Boys, please choose. Choose to explore, to be involved, to engage, and choose to be brave when the situation calls for it. Choose to participate actively once you make a commitment and to be okay with making mistakes. You won't do everything perfectly. However, you won't do *anything* if you don't interact. Being open and available and choosing to be engaged can truly enrich your life and help the world feel like a smaller and more welcoming place.

Wherever the intersections lead you, my hope is that you'll receive the right connections, arrive on time, navigate choices correctly, and ultimately follow the right path. Whatever the outcome of the many intersections you travel, whether that means success or a lesson learned that serves you well in the future, I am praying at the "intersections" for you and hope you are praying too. I am so blessed that we intersected.

God bless you!

Mom

Ginger Shelhimer has travelled all the paths a woman, friend, mother, daughter, mentor, teacher, trainer, human resources professional, and corporate executive can take, and has been very fortunate to always arrive at great and blessed intersections.

Be Kind, Mind Your Words

Dear Ethan and Hannah,

One activity I miss most about your childhood days is reading together. Those times, for me, were about sharing one of the things I love most—books—with two of the people I love most: each of you. Even as toddlers you would recite entire lines because we read so often such favourites as Bill Martin Jr., Dr. Seuss, Eric Carle, Jane Dyer, Margaret Wise Brown, and Mem Fox. Once in a while, a snippet of a story will resurface in our reminiscing; I like to think it's because stories have a way of taking residence in us. I know lots of those stories still live in me, and I hope they live in you, too. I started reading to each of you even before you were born, hoping the sound of my voice would settle in deeply, take root, like the stories. From board books to picture books, from illustrated chapter books to novels (sometimes with strong language): they were all fodder for focused time and conversation with each of you, and a chance to peer into imagined lives.

Now that you are both teenagers, or nearly so, we don't seem to take the same kind of concentrated quiet time to spend together. You are each preoccupied with growing up, becoming your own person, while I am trying to refrain from holding you back too much. The impulse is only to protect you, of course, although I know it feels more malevolent to you than caring, at times. It's difficult to understand how "not yet," "not this time," and "no" express love and concern for you. I hope that by my showing an abiding regard for your well-being you will learn to set the bar for yourselves, too: how you see your place in the world—you matter—and also to care about the well-being of others.

We talk a lot these days—and did even before your teenage years—about the impact of language on the people around us, and what our chosen words reveal about ourselves and communicate to others. Words carry power: they can build us up or tear us down, and they can easily relay something other than what we intend. (We've had enough misunderstandings and misspoken words to make my case!) We all have said things we wish we could take back, reframe, or explain differently. Of course, none of us is perfect, but remember: a sincere apology can help set things right.

When I encourage you to be mindful of your words, what I mean is to take the other person's perspective into account: consider how what you say will make that person feel. Along with books (art in general, really), relationships are the treasures of life. We can build strong, healthy, happy relationships with kind words. I am not promising relationships will always be easy or that they will always last, but I know that kind words (and kind actions, too!) build a strong foundation for our connection with others.

I keep a little green pitcher that belonged to my maternal grand-mother on our kitchen windowsill (the one we keep the lip balm in); it bears the motto, *say a kind word when you can.* When I fall short in setting the example, that little green pitcher reminds me, through its historic connection to halcyon days with all my grandparents, how important I was to them. With kind and caring words, they told me so. And after all these years without them, that is what I remember best. I was fortunate to have their influence in my life, however short the time, because I learned from them, just as I learned from my parents, the absolute necessity for kind words; they can make all the difference to our sense of self and to how we treat others.

This brings me back to our story time. Sure, we explored other people's stories then—Henkes and Lofting, Milne and Sendak—but we were making our own stories together, too; nourishing our relationship and making happy memories. This is the beauty of the power of words and why kind ones are essential: words can bring us closer together, words can help us to understand one another and the world we live in, and words can help make the world a better place—if we choose them mindfully, with kindness. Wherever your own journeys take you, I hope the kind words I utter to you, carried on the sound of my voice, accompany you always.

Much love,

Mum xoxo

Paula Sarson enjoys working with words as a freelance editor. Just before the arrival of her firstborn in 1998, she chose to build her life around family, which has since expanded beyond an extraordinary, supportive husband and two wonderful, humorous teens to include two adorable, zany dogs and three sociable cats.

Playground Wisdom:
Life Lessons from My Toddlers

Dear Kate and Luke,

*L*ife is an adventure.

Your joy-seeking dad has been teaching me to look at life that way. Adventures can be thrilling, a little scary, boundary testing, skill-building and perspective-giving. And I think people are smart or lucky (or both) in life, if they have a sense of some key moments they want to experience along the way. While I have not known all of the harbours I would stop at—and of course the not knowing is part of the fun—I did know one thing: I knew that I wanted to meet you and to be your mother. And that is the gift that you have both given me, the chance to arrive at one of the most important points in my adventure: motherhood. The best part of arriving at this point is the fact that both of you are coming with me for the rest of the way. I am overjoyed by the love that I have for you and am grateful for how much you have already changed my life for the better.

Wisdom may not always be gained from years of experience. Sometimes it may simply be about having another perspective. You are both wise. You came into this world with beautifully simple practices that have taught me some important skills to help me thrive for the second half of my life adventure. I am sharing them with you here so that you can use them as a guide when you may need reminding of what really matters.

Live in the moment as often as you can. I love watching you play with each other, laughing or throwing the ball or chasing each other around the family room. While you remember the past and you think about exciting things in the future, mostly you focus on how we can be enjoying now. Use the past as a guide, but let it go when it does not serve you well. And use the future as a concept map, not an actual map. Understand that if you generally know the direction in which you are travelling, you may just end up in some places that are more amazing than you thought possible.

Hold hands. When you are sick, or sad, or happy, hold someone's hand. I just spent the night in your room, Kate, while you were running a high fever. And you reached out to hold my hand. In that exchange, I know we were both comforted. Holding hands teaches you to know when to ask for help, to reach for what you need, to be connected and to share mutual caring. In life you need to know how to care for others, how to care for yourself, and (the hard part) how to be cared for. When you grow up, please do not forget how to be taken care of by those you love.

Say what you need to say. Be clear in your communication and say what you need. From the beginning, Luke, you have known how to be direct. You signalled and gestured before you spoke any words. You would rub your eyes, shake your head from side to side, open your mouth and press it against mine for a kiss, or come over to rest your head on my lap. And it is so easy to be with you, because you just say what you need. No one is going to look out for you better than you. Be true to yourself, listen to your instincts, and tell people what you need to say.

Be nice to each other. Having a sibling is the best. And you may not know that until you are older. Until you are moving along in your career, choosing a life partner, or creating new friendships, you may not understand that siblings help you to learn how to negotiate, how to share, how to laugh so hard you snort chocolate milk out through your nose. Both of you instinctively comfort one another. Luke crawls over to you, Kate, when you are sad and pats your head. And when Luke was first home from the hospital, Kate, you would sing "Twinkle, Twinkle" every time he started to cry. Even now, he stops crying when his sweet big sister breaks into that song. Being considerate, thoughtful, and understanding of others is rewarding. Practice with each other and all of your other interactions with people in life will be made easier—if you are nice to each other.

Celebrate. Sing and dance. Sing even when you do not know the words. Luke, you are too young to know the lyrics, but when Kate and I sing, you join in, making the tune with your sweet hums. And we all smile. Do things because they feel good, and you will get better and better. Have dance parties in the kitchen when the mood hits you. Kate, you dance and move and sway whenever and wherever you feel like it. I hope you will always make the time to do the things that you are moved to do.

Believe. The wonder, the excitement, and the commitment to what you believe is so simple and so powerful. If you can believe in something great, it will carry you through to make that belief become a reality. Decide what you believe and don't give up on it. And always delight in the magic and beauty of life because it is always all around you—even when you are having trouble seeing it.

Play. This one needs no explanation.

Do not be afraid to make mistakes; learning comes from making them. Watching you both grow, I am reminded that part of the process of mastering any skill is doing it over and over and always requires that you make a few mistakes along the way. You bump and fall, trip and get scrapes. Please do not ever be afraid of making mistakes.

Slow down. When you were born, time seemed to drift away and I resided in a foggy, beautiful place that was fully connected to the moment. And during the first year of each of your lives, I noticed everything: the blossoms coming out day by day on the tree; the leaves swirling in the autumn air; each coo and yawn of newborn babes. There are moments in your life when time stands still. And I am beginning to think that you are succeeding in life the more often you are able to have those moments.

Kate, we had a day when you had finally mastered how to blow countless bubbles. The sky was bright blue, the bubbles danced around us, and we laughed and chased each other. And all I can see when I close my eyes and think of that day is the happiness in your eyes. And Luke, we roll, and tickle, and snuggle, and laugh. And I am solely focused on your next giggle and delight. Everything slows down because we are experiencing joy together. Take time to slow down and practice it often.

Love your family. Unconditionally. Always. You have one family, and when everything is going well, family matters. When you need your family or there is an inevitable challenge in life, your family is there for you. And you need to be there for your family. They are your team. Your clan. Your crew. Love them. Family teaches you that while you are different and may not see eye to eye, you can still practice the art of loving people unconditionally. And you are lucky to have a family that will, unconditionally, love you back.

Thank you for being my guides. I hope this letter will keep you grounded in those simple, beautiful things you both do every day that make it such a joy to be your mother. I've waited my whole life to go on your first field trip, to bake gingerbread cookies together, to teach you songs to sing, and to rock you each to sleep. Thank you for giving me that opportunity. And know that I am eager to support you on the pursuits that matter most to you along your adventure, because loving you and helping you, in some small way, to chart your own adventure is a joy and responsibility that I take very seriously.

I will love you forever and always,

Mommy

P. S. Wear sunscreen and a hat. And take a sweater in case it gets cool at night.

Nicole Beben-Walterhouse is a mother, wife, sister, daughter, aunt, friend, and colleague who prides herself most on her relationships. She married her best friend and is grateful for her healthy, amazing kids. She has worked within the health and telecom sectors for fifteen years and is currently a vice-president in the home health care sector.

Grow to be the Change the World Needs

To my children,

Please let me share a few words of wisdom and life lessons with you. Reread them, let them sink in and please apply them to your own life when your journey finds you at a crossroads.

I have loved each of you from the moment I found out that I was expecting you. There is no greater call than that of a parent. None of you came with handbooks and each of you came with your own personality and traits.

To this day my greatest accomplishment is my children. I hope I have given you roots and wings throughout your years. Roots because it is always important to know from where you came. Keep in touch with your family, for it will always be the one true root in your life. I've given you roots so that you'll know, firm in your heart, what is true, and that your morals and values are such that you are of stalwart character. Wings because I have taught you to have faith in yourselves, to pursue your dreams and enjoy the journey of personal growth we call life.

Please remember that there is no mistake in life if you have learned a lesson from it.

There will come times in your life when you will walk away from all the drama and people who create it—it is like acid to your soul—and you will surround yourself with people who make you laugh, forget the bad, and focus on the good. Love the people who treat you right and pray for the ones who don't. Life truly is too short to be anything less than happy. Falling down is part of life, but getting up is living. My hope is that you will grow up and strive to be:

Prayerful: in searching for guidance within yourself and in your life

Kind: everyone you meet is fighting a battle you know nothing about

Humble: always be able to determine a need versus a want

Loving: to love everyone may be difficult; start by loving yourself

Honest: with yourself, with others, and in all dealings you make

Forgiving: always forgive but never forget the lesson learned. Ask for
forgiveness to make a wrong, right

Of service: the lessons and personal growth you will experience will be
ten times greater than you imagined

Sincere: in your speech, actions, and thoughts

Real: be consistent in your character. Be true to who you truly are and
the family name you bear

A booster: continue to be that dose of sunshine for everyone you meet.

The love I have for you, my children, is one that is difficult to form into words, but I hope that simply by serving you, teaching you, worrying about you, and praying for each of you daily, that you all have felt just how much I love you!

May you all grow to be the change the world needs.

For now, forever and always,

Your Mother

Andrea L. (Davison) Pahulu is a loving mom and caring partner. She has travelled and lived all over the world from New Zealand and Tonga to Canada's North and the USA. She is inspired to share a faith-driven life and be an active part of her children's lives.

Thank You for the Privilege of Being Your Mother

Parker and Taylor:

*Y*esterday I attended the funeral of a bright young man. In so many ways, he reminded me of you. He had caring friends, loving parents, and a sister who adored him. The ceremony was beautiful. Just the right words were said, inspirational music was played, and the sanctuary was full. And it took everything I had to stay there.

It physically hurt to be in the room. The congregation felt the deep loss of losing someone who had so much potential. We shared a feeling of vulnerability and recognized this tragedy could happen to one of our children. In every photograph shown, I could imagine your faces. His family's pictures are nearly identical to those in our scrapbooks.

What grieves me most is witnessing the care his mom and dad took to keep him safe. Their pictures affirmed their love in subtle ways: training wheels on his first bike, a helmet fastened under his chin in another, and a life jacket worn as a boat towed him around a lake. This young man was raised "right." He grew up surrounded by a good church home and friends who had similar values. His family took him camping and on family vacations. He was involved in activities like orchestra and scouting. When he needed extra attention in school or with life, his parents found the help just like we have done with you.

Your dad and I have given you the best guidance, support, education, and opportunities we've known. Despite heroic efforts and tough decisions, this family lost their precious child. Despite best-laid plans, worrying, and occasional nagging, nothing will keep you safe or force you to make the best choices. Your futures are defined by both circumstances outside your control and the choices you make around those situations you can. The best we can do as parents is hope and pray.

I hope and pray you will:

Make decisions that benefit you while benefiting the world around you. Those who get ahead being selfish and thoughtless usually end up alone or with people they can't trust.

Choose to make your marks on this planet with your unique talents. There is absolutely no one in this world quite like you, and no one could ever take your place.

Encourage others and have the courage to say "no" when you know the actions don't fit you or your beliefs. Being supportive doesn't mean supporting bad decisions or a path you know is wrong.

Judge what makes sense for you and stop being concerned about how others might judge you. Your journeys may be similar, may simply intersect, or may travel in opposite ways.

Assume others acted with best intentions and forgive slights where possible. Your lives will be richer if you are not always concerned about others cheating you and if you let go of the little things.

Challenge yourselves to be better, yet control the desire to be perfect in all things. You'll make mistakes and won't complete everything. Learn and apply what works toward your next challenge.

Invest in yourselves. Be a constant learner and stay curious. If you receive an opportunity, advice, or a job, someone has invested in you. Repay that investor with hard work, your best efforts, and respect.

Be someone of character without mischaracterizing others. Make your word your bond. Act so that others can trust you. Don't ruin their faith in you by spreading lies, rumours, or gossip.

Treat people with kindness. We don't know a person's history or personal struggles. Yours may be the only smile or thoughtful word they receive that day, that week, or that month.

Show respect without regard to status, age, or background. "Please" and "thank you" are underrated; manners are valuable and create opportunities that thoughtlessness can't touch.

Offer help freely. Self-sufficiency is overrated. It is a privilege to offer assistance. And don't be stubborn or deny others the gift and opportunity to help you when you need aid.

Have confidence and help others assert their viewpoints. You were raised with a sense of self-awareness and have communication skills. Others may need encouragement to express their thoughts or feelings.

Make sure that your goals have enough risk and challenge to keep you interested, but aren't so risky as to damage your health, relationships, or financial tolerance.

Find someone amazing to share your life, someone who inspires you to be amazing and to be the best you can in all situations. Nurture a loving relationship as deep and supportive as your father's and mine.

God gave you to Dad and me for a reason.

No one will ever care as much about your well-being or give you advice with your best interests at heart as we will. We've prayed for you, cheered for you, and fought for you. No matter how great your accomplishments or how bad you may feel about your mistakes, we love you unconditionally, forever.

There would be no greater gift than being granted the opportunity to see you grown and making a positive difference in the world. I hope and pray you are able to experience the gift of having incredible children like we have in you. Journey on with purpose and joy; continue making a positive impact on others. You have so much to offer this world. Thank you for the privilege of being your mother.

Love you always,

Mom

Linda Byars Swindling is a "recovering attorney," an author, and a business owner. She works with organizations on negotiation strategies that drive high performance. Her personal-development company, Journey On, is based on the belief that our experiences add to our life's journey and to God's purpose for us. Her biggest negotiation and communication lessons come from her family, including husband, Gregg, and their teens, Parker and Taylor.

You are Wise Beyond Your Years

To my Reesie bug,

*L*ittle kids are often asked, "What you want to be when you grow up?" Pictures of their dreams are drawn and coloured in primary school and as they ascend into higher grades, essays are written outlining their goals in life, aspirations of career paths, and things like how many children they would like to have. Having just turned forty, I still find myself reflecting on this question. What do I want to do? What kind of person am I? What kind of person do I want to be? And it occurred to me one day when I was watching you play that I want to be like you.

At three years old you have already endured hardships that could span a lifetime. You were desperately sick with life-threatening leukemia. You were torn from my arms to undergo painful and frightening medical procedures. You were poisoned with chemotherapy, isolated from your family and the outdoors. You underwent a bone marrow transplant and were essentially robbed of half your life. And yet your sweet, innocent soul was left unscathed.

You see beauty in everything. It is such a treat for us to take you to new places and watch your eyes light up and hear you marvel, "Oh Mommy, this place is so beautiful and amazing." It doesn't seem to matter if you are seeing something old, elegant, drab, or colourful: if you haven't seen it before, you are spellbound.

You are resilient. I tell anyone who asks, "Reese got me though this." One especially difficult day at SickKids hospital in Toronto, I burst in to uncontrollable sobs. You and I were living in a ten-by-ten isolation room while we waited for your new immune system to mature, and the strain and worry overwhelmed me. I broke down emotionally. It was the first time in a year that you had seen me cry. You were startled initially, but then crawled across the hospital bed, placed a hand on either one of my cheeks, and said, "Mommy, you be happy. I okay." You were a week shy of your second birthday, intuitive and wise beyond your years.

You are generous. You break chocolate bars in half to share with your older brother and offer him the biggest piece.

You are empathic. At the pool one day you saw a woman who did not have any hair; she was a breast cancer survivor. You waded over to her and said kindly, "Don't you worry...it will all grow back." At the IWK, while we were waiting for your turn to see the oncologist, you comfort the other worried, frightened patients. I have seen you leave the play area to track a crying child to an examining room where you try to calm him down by describing a checkup and blood work to him.

Reese, you exude joy. You dance, sing, and smile at the world. When we go for walks together you turn heads. I believe people see you as a ray of light, skipping along the sidewalk.

You have turned your lemons into lemonade. It would be so easy, even at your tender age, to be scarred by the hand you were dealt. But instead you have emerged as the epitome of human kindness. Your spirit is that of unconditional joy and innocence. You appreciate every day.

My advice to you, Reese, would be to not change. Life will throw more curveballs at you and you will experience hardship, but do not allow circumstance to change the core of your being. Grow, mature, discover what makes you happy; be angry, be sad, but always remember that three-year-old who was crushed physically by leukemia two times, but whose courageous, loving spirit triumphed. Do not let the difficult times define you. Continue to inspire others to live by your example.

I love you and cherish every day we are together.

Mommy

Kora Hanrahan is a loving mother and partner. She has grown while standing alongside her son, Reese, who underwent the rigours of leukemia treatment as a very young child. Kora loves to run and travel, and spends much of her volunteer time raising money to help end cancer.

Letter to My Daughter

A,

Right now, you're almost ten months old. I have known you for twice that time, nestled under my ribs, growing from a moment into a person. Right now, you are chubby wrists, peach fuzz, ringlets, a big grin with two teeth. I wish I could have you like this always, and watch you grow at the same time. Who will you be in ten years, in twenty, in fifty? What I wish for you is this: that you retain much of what makes you a delight right now.

I hope you'll have the same enthusiasm you do today. You literally throw yourself at the world, fearless, not knowing you might fall off the sofa, off the steps, into the shower door, without someone there to hang on to you. You can't contain your excitement: you flap your arms and babble when you see the next wonderful thing. I hope you throw yourself into each wonderful thing you find.

The sense of wonder I see in your eyes, flaring wide with interest as you encounter the new, is the gift of a lifetime. I hope you retain the sense of curiosity you have now—it is one of the virtues I value most in your father. You will never be bored when you bring to your life this sense of desire, this need to understand, this sense that everything in the world is infinitely worth investigating, assessing, and knowing.

I hope you always have the same immense capacity for joy you do now: the sheer delight that animates your face, that lights your eyes with mischief. Your baby-laugh burbles loud and often, and you see the world as a place that might offer new joys every moment. I hope it does. And when grand moments of happiness aren't to be had, I hope you will find warmth and contentment in daily living, always seeing it new.

I wish with all my being that you'll find people who love you like we do—fiercely, laughingly, and patiently, with more space in our hearts than we knew we had—throughout all your life. I can't imagine not being near you, finding such joy just watching the expressions on your face. I want so much for you to be happy, and so I want you to be surrounded by people who feel just as we do, always.

Lastly, I hope you'll love the people in your life the way you do now: with a sense of happy discovery every time you see them; with arms up and outstretched, ready to embrace; with innate kindness and interest, bringing light and warmth wherever you are. Know that you are a gift to me and to everyone else you meet.

Love,

Mom

Susanne Marshall is a writing advisor at Dalhousie University. She is drawn to the magic of Paris and to building romance with the love of her life. She was recently blessed with a magnificent daughter with whom she enjoys spending time at the beach, exploring the outdoors and great books.

Message in a Bottle

For my children,

I am getting to be "of a certain age," as the French say, when you think about the legacy you want to leave behind for your loved ones. Throughout my journey, I have discovered three things that have helped me create a fulfilling life. I may not be on my deathbed just yet, but I wanted to share these insights with you in the hope that they may offer some guidance and encouragement.

1. Invest in others

There is no greater joy than to contribute what you have to others. For me, this is a talent for coaching in the business environment. For you, it may be your music, the way you cook, your ability to help hone the athletic skills of others. It's not the "what" that you contribute, but the heart that you bring to it and your commitment to others that matters most. Give wholeheartedly and selflessly and you will have a deep satisfaction in your life that cannot compare to anything else.

Once, I attended a company conference after coaching its company's president through some difficult issues the year before. His grown daughter came up to me and thanked me for my work with her father, which had focused in part on his ability to listen and connect with his team. She told me with tears in her eyes that she now had a relationship with him for the first time in her life. I was touched, and deeply thankful for the opportunity to have worked with him and to see how it impacted his family. It reminded me that investing in others has a ripple effect that benefits those close to them as well.

There have also been times when I felt frustrated or powerless in helping someone, but then suddenly he or she started to blossom and I could see the fruit of my labour.

Give your part of the fertilizer to prepare the soil, and remember that sometimes the growth happens later.

2. Follow Your Dreams

This advice is common, and yet so few people actually follow it. It is true that some of us have to explore many paths before finding the one that is most fulfilling and that best fits our talents. That was certainly the case for me.

I was uncertain about my path in my twenties. I was driven by an inner need to find "my work"—the way I would express myself in life—but I wasn't sure what I wanted to do. I could not be satisfied with merely a paycheque, nor could I settle for a position that offered security if it didn't also allow me to develop talents I cared about.

I graduated with an English degree and a minor in secondary education. Afterward I tried teaching, both at the high school and college level. I also tried sales and marketing positions where my people skills could help sell a product or service. I liked being with people and having freedom in my schedule, so I knew I was getting closer.

Soon after, I joined an organization devoted to personal growth in which I was trained to lead seminars and also recruit members. Things started to click as I used my people skills and also helped people grow in meaningful ways. One of the former leaders of that organization invited me to work for her small consulting company and she mentored me as a coach and business consultant to small and mid-sized companies. I developed a successful track record in helping owners build effective corporate cultures, high performing teams and profitable growth. A few years later I started my own firm and expanded my services to include strategic planning.

For me, one opportunity led to another—even after I found my calling. You, too, will find your way, as long as you keep looking and learning from past experiences.

3. Seek Help

When you are stuck, find help! Without seeking help, you will not be able to overcome your weaknesses and will never fulfill your potential. As I look back, the hardest times were when I thought I had to go it alone and did not seek support.

One of my biggest mistakes was to not finish the thesis for my MBA program. At the end of three years of coursework I was required to write a one hundred-page thesis summarizing what I had learned, applied to a business case. I didn't fully understand how to approach that project and was frankly overwhelmed by the other things going on in my life. I did not ask for help, and set my thesis aside.

At age twenty-nine, I moved across the country to Dallas and got caught up in starting a new life there. Shortly after, my mother died, followed by my father a year later. It was a sad and lonely time. I was new to a city where I didn't know anyone, unsure of my career path, and grieving the death of both parents. I never completed my thesis and later discovered that it was too late to get my MBA without repeating the entire program.

There were several hard lessons. The obvious one: don't procrastinate. But the deeper lesson is to realize that when you are struggling, it's a sign you need the resources that others can provide. There is no shame in "not knowing" how to do something, especially during a season of change and loss.

I applied that lesson many times over as I built my family and career. I truly learned the power of getting help twenty years later when my marriage failed. It was the second most painful period of my life, but this time I sought out friends, counselors, and my church. I fervently sought God's help and He came through in a big way. Even though it was a very hard time, my relationship with God grew deeper, and it gave me the courage and the wisdom I needed to emerge from the experience with new levels of emotional growth, richer friendships, and a thriving business. Eventually I also remarried and found true happiness with my soulmate, Rod. The help I received made it possible for me to heal, make good decisions, start over, and find fulfillment.

So, kids, I hope you live fully, extracting every bit of your passion, talent, and creativity to offer others everything you have. Don't be afraid to explore, and don't settle. Seek out God with passion and He will guide you well, pull you up when you are down, and send you just the right people to provide the support you need to grow.

A famous quote from Erma Bombeck, who was my mother's favourite humourist and columnist, encompasses my wish for you: "When I stand before God at the end of my life, I would hope that I would not have a single bit of talent left and could say, 'I used everything you gave me.'"

Love,

Mama/Mijah/Grammy/Aunt E

Elaine Morris is a master-level emotional intelligence coach. She works to help leaders access deeper growth and personal awareness by connecting authentically, inspiring team insights and building decisions that produce winning strategies. Elaine loves to decompress with Pilates, yoga, and group weight classes with lots of loud music. She lives in Dallas with her husband, Rod, and together they enjoy motorcycling on country roads and spending time with their kids Julia and Sam in Chicago, and Jeaneen and Cosmo (and grandson, Connor) in Dallas. Visit her at elainemorris.com.

You Don't Know What You Want Until You've Got It

Dear Dylan, Quinn, and Jillian,

*A*s I've been thinking about writing this, I've been struggling with what message I would leave in a bottle for you if I only had eight hundred words to tell you what being your mother means to me. Would I impart life lessons and advice, or would I tell you how you make me feel? I decided that this will probably be a little of both.

The first thing I want you to know is that being a parent is hard! It's cliché to say that it's rewarding and the most important job in the world. It is those things, and I love you all with my whole heart forever and ever, but it's also a lot of work! It is, by far, the most difficult thing I've ever done or will ever do. Nobody really tells you about that.

It's not just the day-to-day stuff that makes it challenging; it's the uncertainty that knocks me out. So much of parenting is hoping for the best: hoping your dad and I have set a good example, hoping we've loved you enough, hoping we've been tough enough. I think it's going pretty well so far, but the years will tell what kind of people you will grow into and I feel a lot of the time that all I can do is hope for the best. That's the unbelievably tough part. Waiting to see if we did it right, if we did a good job in this enormous, important task of raising you three.

When I was young I didn't want to have kids. I used to say, so very earnestly, that it was because I didn't want to contribute to world population growth. But it was really because I was scared to death! I'd had a difficult relationship with my folks and I didn't want to go through that again on the other end. As tough as my teenage years were on me, they were at least that tough on my mother. Yuck! Again, on the flip side? Really?

Then, I met a man who rocked my world and changed my mind. Your dad was a two-for-one deal for me. He came with a three-year-old and a special perspective. I saw what a difference a committed, loving partnership makes to huge life decisions. I hadn't really known that before. How secure it made me feel. Secure enough to jump feet-first into this crazy, wonderful family and create two more amazing people to join the one I was blessed to have picked up along the way.

You are almost through childhood; one of you all the way, the other two well into your teenage years. Each of you has such a wonderfully unique personality. You each are so gifted at different things, and I am amazed at what individuals you are. I am glad that all three of you are so kind. I don't know for sure if we had anything to do with that, but I am really proud. Enormously proud.

You all know that threes are big for me. I am one of three children in my first family, I have an annoying habit of writing in clauses of three, and I have three kids. So, here's another, three things that I've distilled all my parenting advice into: take care of yourself, your space, and your work. I really do believe that these three simple things are the foundation to all I've tried to teach you. Taking care of you means being attuned to your health, diet, hygiene, and fitness. Taking care of your space is being responsible for your stuff and place, whether that is your home in the future, or your room in our home. Because I know you all so well, I know that having a place in the world you can be proud of will always comfort you. Taking care of you work is doing the best job at whatever task is in front of you, whether that is a real job or it is school, hockey, horseback riding. Professional satisfaction is important.

One last thing: consider others in all that you do. Connecting and taking care of the people around you in a gracious manner is the single most important key to a happy life. I hope I've shown you that in practice. I hope, I hope, I hope.

This is really what I hope for you, my three beautiful children: be happy, find true love, and when you're all grown up, visit your old Mom and Dad once in a while.

Love,

Mom

Lara Ryan is a consultant specializing in corporate social responsibility. She is extremely lucky to work on interesting projects for great clients from a home office overlooking the ocean, in a wardrobe that now consists almost entirely of yoga pants, and to have a commute that involves stepping over the dog.

About the Editor

Tyler Hayden is an international leadership and team consultant, elected government official, and founder of the Message in a Bottle book series. He has over two decades of experience as a speaker and organizational consultant and is the author of more than a dozen books and measures on personal development, leadership, and team-building. These are just some of the reasons why Tyler is regularly chosen for leadership and team events internationally.

As one meeting planner said, "Tyler had us at 'Hello.' He is pure energy and you can't help but hang on every word....[We] only wish we'd had more time with him."

You will quickly see why Tyler consistently scores as the top keynote speaker at conferences and meetings from health care and government to oil and gas and banking—Tyler knows how to deliver just-in-time and on-target learning in an engaging and inspiring way. His trademark "Livin' Life Large" leaves audiences with actionable items, custom learning, and a sore belly from laughing so hard.

Tyler's team-building repertoire includes high-adventure activities, virtual team tool kit, on-site adventures, unique professional measures, and more. You'll have to check out his list of team design tools from secret agent movie trailers and off-the-wall Olympics games to cardboard arcades and retro game shows. His team events blend knowledge development and team skills with hilarious fun and out-of-the-box innovation.

You may meet Tyler as your keynote speaker solution. Then, like many, you will engage him in helping to build customized solutions in the areas of leadership development, virtual and on-site team-building, personal development, structured mentoring, and staff retention and engagement.

As one YPO member said, "You were not only able to achieve [our objectives] with exacting detail, but you exceeded every member's expectations."

Some of the success stories he has helped author with clients include: structured mentoring in health care, customer relationship management in IT/IMS, team-building for key account sales, applied research studies, and team-building in virtual and 24-7 work environments. Tyler's thought leadership will help guide innovation, leadership, and team skills within your business for years to come.

Finally, a description of Tyler would not be complete without acknowledging his greatest source of affluence: his family. Tyler is a loving husband to Laurie, a school educator, and "crazy" dad to Tait and Breton, his two beautiful princesses. They are dedicated travellers and adventurers, active community leaders, and animal care enthusiasts. They cherish being part of a loving family and making a difference from their seaside farm in the beautiful town of Lunenburg.

Learn more about Tyler's interactive team-building and keynote services at www.tylerhayden.com.

Do you have a letter to share?

If you are interested in having a letter published in an upcoming Message in a Bottle book, we would love to hear from you!

Our books are written by our expert readers—that means you. So burn up your computer's keyboard and fire us off a letter for an upcoming book. We'd love to consider it for a future publication! We are currently welcoming submissions for upcoming titles including:

~ Grandma's Message in a Bottle

~ Grandpa's Message in a Bottle

~ Sister's Message in a Bottle

~ Brother's Message in a Bottle

~ Kid's Message in a Bottle

~ New Mother's Message in a Bottle

~ New Father's Message in a Bottle

To submit your letter, go to www.messageinabottlebook.com and follow the links.